Memorable Meals
for Family & Friends

ROBERT CARRIER'S KITCHEN

Memorable Meals
for Family & Friends

Marshall Cavendish   London Sydney & New York

Editor	Roz Fishel
Editorial Staff	Caroline Macy
	Penny Smith
	Kate Toner
Designer	Alan White
Series Editor	Pepita Aris
Production Executive	Robert Paulley
Production Controller	Steve Roberts

Photography
Bryce Attwell: 98, 99, 100, 101
Paul Bussell: 15, 37, 45, 67, 74, 106, 108, 109
Alan Duns: 97
Laurie Evans: 26, 32, 38, 47, 54, 57
Robert Golden: 8
Edmund Goldspink: 72, 92
Melvin Grey: 88
James Harris: 105
James Jackson: 10, 18, 36, 42, 56, 79
Paul Kemp: 62
John Kevern: 83
Chris Knaggs: 17, 22, 40, 50, 65, 66, 68, 78, 84, 87, 90, 102, 104, 110
Don Last: 85
David Levin: 90, 91
Peter Myers: 2, 13, 16, 20, 24, 34, 44, 46, 49, 51, 52, 55, 58, 76, 78, 79, 83, 86, 92, 94, 96, 97, 99, 100, 103, 105
Paul Webber: 70
Paul Webster: 18
Paul Williams: 11, 28, 30, 80, 82, 86
Cover picture: **Peter Myers**

Weights and measures
Both metric and imperial measurements are given. As these are not exact equivalents, please work from one set of figures or the other. Use graded measuring spoons levelled across.

Time symbols
The time needed to prepare the dish is given on each recipe. The symbols are as follows:

 simple to prepare and cook

 straightforward but requires more skill or attention

 time-consuming to prepare or requires extra skill

 must be started 1 day or more ahead

On the cover: Guinea fowl with fresh fruits, page 96

This edition published 1985
© Marshall Cavendish Limited 1985

Printed in Italy by
L.E.G.O. S.p.a. Vicenza

Typeset by Quadraset Limited, Midsomer Norton, Bath, Avon

Published by Marshall Cavendish House
58 Old Compton Street London W1V 5PA
ISBN 0 86307 264 X (series)
ISBN 0 86307 404 9 (this volume)

Contents

Brighten up your everyday cooking for the family with the help of this excellent volume. *Memorable Meals for Family & Friends* is packed with imaginative ideas not only for feeding the family but also for when you entertain friends. Dishes range from the very casual to the more formal, and I have catered for a wide range of age groups and tastes.

In my section 'The Clever Cook', there are ideas on how to double-up the dinner if more people arrive than you were expecting; how to organize food to be served quickly after you get home from a day out; and a few ways to 'cheat' in the kitchen so you can produce delicious meals like Spinach roulade and Ginger cream log in a minimum amount of time — a bonus if you have guests, since it will allow you to spend more time with them and not in the kitchen.

If you need an economy week, I include budget recipes for main meals and desserts. Try my exciting recipes for using left-over chicken (sherry-flavoured Chicken pancakes amandine, for instance), or transform ordinary mince into a superb meal like Gourmet hamburgers. Sometimes a hearty soup and fresh bread are the answer to a substantial meal, and I have included a section on nourishing and tasty soups. Quick cheese soup or Gardeners' soup are among the more unusual suggestions.

Today, many cooks have time-saving appliances such as pressure cookers, food processors, microwave ovens and freezers, so I have included individual sections on all of this equipment to help you use it to the best possible advantage. The sweet and savoury dishes you can create are quite irresistible.

If you have guests staying for the weekend, my chapter on Two-tier meals is invaluable. For instance, serve the children Tomato-painted chicken legs for supper, then — using the chicken breasts — make a sophisticated dinner party dish, such as Chicken turnovers, for the adults.

I have also included suggestions for complete three-course meals, although of course you may prefer to devise your own menus from the recipes in the other chapters. I have aimed to provide a wide variety of tempting starters, main course dishes and desserts to suit different occasions, from a hearty family meal to a gourmet dinner party. Follow my useful Plan-ahead timetables which will help to ensure that all the preparation goes as smoothly as possible.

Happy cooking and bon appétit!

Robert Carrier

Budget Cookery

SOUPS FOR ALL OCCASIONS

Served with chunks of bread and cheese, a hot, hearty soup makes a perfect midday snack or supper for the family. Easy to make, and capable of great variety, these warming soups are also wonderfully economical.

Most soups involve very little effort: the majority of recipes are quite simple to make but in any case, should you make errors along the way, they can easily be corrected. Too thick? Add water, milk or cream. Too thin? Thickeners will take care of that. No time to chop vegetables? A few seconds in the blender can change cooked vegetables into a lovely, creamy soup.

A soup can be something that is uniquely yours. Many cooks agree that some of the best soups are those simply put together from leftovers, never to be repeated. Pleasing yourself is the only rule. A look in your refrigerator is usually the start, but you can use ingredients from packets and the contents of the freezer as well.

Soup bases

If you have some stock to hand you are halfway to making soup. Although stock cubes are marvellous time-savers, it is better to use a well-flavoured home-made stock. Left-over beef bones — preferably browned first with vegetables — and simmered vegetables make excellent stocks, as do all poultry carcasses simmered in water. Pork and lamb bones are less suitable.

The stock left over from cooking a ham, bacon joint or a tongue tends to be very salty: use it in proportion one third to two thirds other liquids. The stock left over from boiling a chicken is also an ideal base for a soup.

A stock made from the peelings and other scraps of washed vegetables makes a very cheap soup base. Use the outer leaves of lettuces, the green ends of leeks, onion skins (which colour the soup brown), the coarser stalks and the leaves of celery, and watercress and parsley stalks.

Traditionally, the liquid used for cooking vegetables became the basis for tasty, nutritious soups; for instance, bean water is particularly good, and cauliflower water, which has quite a strong flavour, combines well with parsnips for parsnip soup.

Soup tips

● Vegetables which are past their prime are good candidates for soup. Chop them and add them to a well-flavoured stock. Or chop and sauté them in oil, then simmer them in water until they are tender. Blend or purée them through a vegetable mill or sieve, re-heat and season.
● For speeding up the process, do not forget the pressure cooker (see page 68) — stocks can be made in a much shorter time and vegetables, meat and pulses can be cooked in liquid in almost no time at all.
● For thickening up a watery soup, make a *beurre manié* (a paste made with equal parts of butter and flour) and whisk it into the simmering soup a little at a time. Or whisked in, cubed, left-over boiled potatoes or a

little instant potato powder can also do the trick.
● Two spoonfuls of rice or any small pasta add body to a soup. Try using semolina, or sago for a different texture.
● To add a touch of luxury to white soup, stir in a few tablespoons of single cream, or even canned cream — the preserved taste is removed by cooking.
● To pad out a soup, add concentrated canned or packet soups. Remember, these are already seasoned so add sufficient liquid to balance the flavour.
● To increase the flavour, blend in a stock cube. Or stir in some sherry, wine, dry Marsala, or dry white martini — even a little wine vinegar if you are discreet about the amount you add.
● Any leftovers can be used to make a soup more substantial — for instance meat trimmings from a joint, cooked vegetables, cooked pasta and rice.
● Most soups freeze well, but use herbs and spices sparingly and avoid adding garlic before freezing — add after thawing. Cream, eggs or milk should not be included before freezing as these can cause curdling — add them at the reheating stage. Soups and stock bases will also store well in the refrigerator, usually for up to 5 days.

Soup garnishes

● For a crunchy garnish, cut stale white bread into cubes and fry it to make crunchy, golden croûtons. Or grill 2 slices of bacon until crisp and then crumble it on top before serving.
● For cold soups a swirl of cream, a floating slice of lemon, watercress leaves and cucumber slices all add style.
● Don't forget fresh parsley: a sprinkling of this herb, finely chopped, is welcome for its colour and taste.

Beef soup with dumplings

The addition of light-weight dumplings turns this soup into a sustaining meal-in-a-bowl.

 45 minutes

Serves 6
1 L /2 pt beef stock, home-made or
   from a cube
100 g /4 oz left-over cooked beef cut into
   bite-sized pieces
1 onion, chopped
3 medium-sized carrots, cleaned and diced
2 medium-sized potatoes, peeled and diced
1 celery stick, cleaned and sliced
salt
freshly ground black pepper

For the dumplings
50 g /2 oz self-raising flour, plus extra for
   dusting
salt and freshly ground black pepper
50 g /2 oz fresh breadcrumbs
50 g /2 oz shredded suet
15 ml /1 tbls freshly chopped mixed herbs
1 small egg, beaten

1 Put the beef stock in a large saucepan and add the beef, onion, carrots, potatoes, celery and salt and pepper. Bring to the boil, then lower the heat and simmer for 20 minutes.
2 Meanwhile, prepare the dumplings: sieve the flour and salt into a large mixing bowl. Mix in the breadcrumbs, suet, herbs and black pepper and make a well in the centre.
3 Pour the beaten egg into the well, then stir and cut through, using a palette knife, until the mixture forms a dough. Knead the dough on a floured surface until it is smooth and free from cracks. Divide the dough into walnut-sized pieces and roll each piece into a ball between your floured palms.
4 Add the dumplings to the pan at the end of the simmering time. Cover with a lid and simmer for a further 10 minutes.
5 Adjust the seasoning and ladle the soup into individual bowls, giving 4–5 dumplings per serving.

● Other root vegetables may be used instead of the carrots and potatoes. Left-over cooked pasta shapes also make a good alternative to the dumplings.

Beef soup with dumplings

Cucumber and courgette soup

 30 minutes

Serves 6
25 g /1 oz butter
1 medium-sized onion, finely chopped
250 g /9 oz cucumber
250 g /9 oz courgettes
1 L /2 pt best-quality canned chicken consommé
salt
freshly ground black pepper
2 eggs
150 ml /5 fl oz thin cream
15 ml /1 tbls freshly chopped parsley or chives

1   Heat the butter in a heavy saucepan over medium heat and sauté the onion until it is soft but not browned.
2   Meanwhile, trim but do not peel the cucumber and courgettes and grate coarsely. Add to the soft onion and cook, stirring, for 1 minute. Pour in the chicken consommé and simmer for 5 minutes.
3   Purée the soup in a blender. Strain the purée, including the lumps, through a fine sieve back into the saucepan. Season to taste and keep the soup hot over a low heat while you prepare the enrichment.
4   In a bowl, whisk together the eggs and the cream. Whisk 200 ml /7 fl oz of the hot soup into the egg and cream mixture, then whisk this creamy mixture into the soup. Cook, stirring, until lightly thickened, but do not boil or the soup will curdle. Garnish with the freshly chopped parsley or chives and serve immediately.

Gardeners' soup

This soup is really a vegetable main meal, often served at midday in France and followed only by cheese.

 45 minutes

Serves 6
about 700 g /1½ lb white cabbage, tough outer leaves removed
the white part of 6 medium-sized leeks
50 g /2 oz lard
500 g /1 lb potatoes, diced
225 g /8 oz shelled or frozen green peas
1 L /1¾ pt chicken stock, home-made or from a cube
15 ml /1 tbls chopped fresh chervil or 5 ml /1 tsp dried chervil
salt and freshly ground black pepper
25 g /1 oz butter
1 small round lettuce, shredded

1   Cut the cabbage into 6 wedges and remove the hard core. Slice the leeks finely.
2   Melt the lard in a large saucepan over a medium heat, add the cabbage and leeks and stir well. Cover and cook for 5 minutes, stirring occasionally.
3   Add the potatoes and peas, the stock, the chervil and then season. Bring the mixture back to the boil, cover and cook gently over a medium-low heat for 20 minutes or until the cabbage wedges are tender.
4   Melt the butter in a frying-pan over high heat, quickly stir in the lettuce and toss for 30 seconds. Add the lettuce to the soup and bring it back to the boil. Adjust the seasoning and then serve.

Turkey soup ad hoc

This very economical soup can be varied by doubling or omitting some of the vegetables. Frozen vegetables may be substituted for the puréed ones and added near the end of the cooking time.

 1 hour

Serves 8
1 turkey carcass, plus any skin and stuffing
100 g /4 oz mixed raw chopped vegetables, including onions, celery with tops, parsnips, carrots, mushrooms
500 g /1 lb tomatoes, fresh or canned
50 g /2 oz rice
2.5 ml /½ tsp ground paprika
freshly chopped parsley
2.5 ml /½ tsp dried thyme
2.5 ml /½ tsp dried chervil
1 bay leaf
1½ chicken stock cubes
salt
freshly ground black pepper
75 g /2 oz left-over cooked vegetables, puréed

1   Place the turkey carcass in a large saucepan. Add the raw vegetables, tomatoes (skinned if you are using fresh ones), rice, paprika, herbs and stock cubes. Pour in 1 L / 2 pt water. Season to taste.
2   Cover the pan and simmer for about 45 minutes, or until the rice is tender. Remove the turkey carcass from the soup. Strip off any meat left on the carcass and return it to the pan. Remove and discard any turkey skin and the bay leaf.
3   If there is fat floating on top of the soup, skim it off with a spoon or by using a double thickness of absorbent paper.
4   Stir in the puréed left-over vegetables and heat the soup through for 15 minutes. Serve immediately.

Quick cheese soup

Serve this 'instant' soup with herb bread for a quick snack.

 15 minutes

Serves 4–6
425 g /15 oz can cream of celery soup
275 ml /10 fl oz beef stock, made with a stock cube
275 ml /10 fl oz milk
100 g /4 oz mature Cheddar cheese, grated
15 ml /1 tbls finely chopped spring onions
15 ml /1 tbls freshly chopped parsley
For the garnish
crisply fried bacon, crumbled into pieces

1   Combine the celery soup, beef stock and milk over low heat. Stir until well incorporated. Add the cheese and stir until melted.
2   Add the onions and chopped parsley. Heat through but do not boil.
3   To serve, ladle the soup into individual bowls and then sprinkle each serving with crumbled bacon.

BUDGET MAIN MEALS

Used imaginatively, as the following recipes show, inexpensive ingredients such as the cheaper meat and fish buys, seasonal vegetables and dairy foods can be turned into excellent main course dishes for the family.

Some people feel that they have not had a 'proper' meal unless they have eaten a large portion of meat accompanied by at least two vegetables, but this can work out to be very expensive. With a little imagination, however, main meals using the cheaper cuts of meat or less meat — or even no meat at all — can be just as appetizing. It pays to be experimental, as the following recipes show. There is no need to make drastic changes in your diet, though, and the money you save on a budget meal will allow you to serve more expensive cuts of meat, like chops or a roast, another day. Also remember that fresh seasonal vegetables are generally more delicious and cheaper in price than canned vegetables.

Making meat go further

You can serve less meat and still produce a nutritious meal if you combine the meat with another, more filling, source of protein. In Italian favourites such as spaghetti bolognese or carbonara, minced beef or bacon is combined with pasta and often cheese as well. Small quantities of meat can be padded out with rice — brown for preference — in risottos, curries and Chinese stir-fry combinations. You can also mix rice and minced beef to stuff vegetables which can then be baked. Tomatoes, peppers and marrows are particularly suitable for treating in this way (see recipe for Spicy stuffed marrow).

Stuffing cheaper cuts of meat, like breast of lamb, with a mixture of breadcrumbs, onions and herbs will make the meat go much further and absorb any excess fat. Breadcrumbs and minced beef can be mixed to make a really delicious meat loaf which you can roast in the oven. The important thing to remember is to use plenty of seasoning and herbs to give your dish an interesting flavour.

When you make a casserole, try using less meat and more root vegetables, topping it all with sliced potatoes. Choose the cheaper stewing cuts, all of which are extremely tasty if cooked slowly over a long time. Shin of beef, pork belly and oxtail are all just as good nutritionally as fillet steaks or expensive joints of meat.

Offal is as cheap as most of the stewing cuts and, as there is very little waste, bear in mind that you can buy smaller quantities per person. Liver and kidneys can be sliced thinly and quickly fried or gently simmered to give rich-gravied stews (see recipe for Kidneys in beer). The art of cooking liver and kidneys beautifully is, in fact, not to overcook them.

Pulses are an extremely good source of cheap protein and combine very well with meat in spicy dishes, such as red kidney beans and minced beef in a chilli-flavoured sauce, or piquant dishes such as haricot beans

cooked in a tomato sauce with pieces of pork. Using soya protein is a good way to pad out a reduced quantity of meat.

Meals without meat

Meatless meals can be an enjoyable experience for all. Eggs, cheese and the cheaper varieties of fish all cost less than meat and are equally nutritious. On the fish side, go for herrings or mackerel (see Mackerel with gooseberry sauce), or use coley — a cheaper white fish — in fish pies and fish cakes. Smoked haddock is often used in small quantities and is therefore an economical buy.

Combinations of eggs and/or cheese with vegetables in eggs florentine, quiches or dishes such as cauliflower cheese are worth remembering. Cheese and tomato tart (see recipe) is a lovely main course dish, served with a large bowl of crisp salad. Other vegetables make very enjoyable main courses when served with a really good cheese sauce: leeks, white cabbage, or a mixture of root vegetables. If you do not want to abandon the taste of meat completely, top the cheese mixture with slices of fried bacon. Bacon-potato bake (see recipe) is a substantial and very tasty family dish. Nuts can also be turned into delicious main meals.

Mackerel with gooseberry sauce

🍴 30 minutes

Mackerel with gooseberry sauce

Serves 4
225 g /8 oz gooseberries
50 g /2 oz sugar
4 small to medium-sized mackerel
25 g /1 oz butter, melted
1 medium-sized egg, beaten
salt
freshly ground black pepper
flat-leaved parsley, to garnish

1 Place the gooseberries in a pan with the sugar. Put over a gentle heat and stew them in their own juice until soft. Remove and press them through a sieve. Heat the grill.
2 Clean the mackerel and remove their heads. Score the sides of each fish 2 or 3 times. Grill them for 15 minutes, brushing the fish with melted butter from time to time and turning them once.
3 A few minutes before the fish are cooked, return the gooseberry purée to the pan, add the beaten egg and reheat it gently, stirring until the sauce has thickened. Season it.
4 Transfer the fish to a warmed serving dish, garnish, and serve with the sauce.

Kidneys in beer

🍴 45 minutes

Serves 4
50 g /2 oz butter
1 medium-sized onion, sliced
1 small green pepper, seeded and chopped
12 lambs' kidneys
25 g /1 oz flour
100 g /4 oz canned tomatoes
275 ml /10 fl oz pale ale
salt and freshly ground black pepper
5 ml /1 tsp Worcestershire sauce
100 g /4 oz mushrooms, sliced

1 Melt the butter over a low heat in a deep frying-pan or large saucepan. Add the onion

and green pepper and cook then until soft.
2 Prepare the kidneys by cutting each one in half. Remove the outer skin (if this hasn't already been done) and snip out all traces of solid white core with scissors. Turn up the heat, add the kidneys to the pan and fry them quickly until they are browned.
3 Turn down the heat and stir in the flour. Gradually add the tomatoes and their juice, followed by the pale ale, stirring to make a smooth gravy. Bring to the boil, season with salt and pepper and add the Worcestershire sauce. Add the sliced mushrooms and then simmer gently for 20 minutes.

Spicy stuffed marrow

 1 hour

Serves 4
40 g /1½ oz brown rice
1 medium-sized marrow
1 medium-sized onion, chopped
1 garlic clove, crushed
65 g /2½ oz butter
225 g /8 oz minced beef
10 ml /2 tsp flour
5 ml /1 tsp cumin
5 ml /1 tsp turmeric
15 ml /1 tbls tomato purée
150 ml /5 fl oz beef stock, home-made or
  from a cube
100 g /4 oz mushrooms, thinly sliced
salt and freshly ground black pepper
butter, for greasing
2 medium-sized tomatoes, sliced

1 Put the brown rice into a measuring cup and note its volume, then transfer it to a saucepan with 2½ times its volume of water. Bring it to the boil, stir once, then cover and simmer for 40–50 minutes, until almost

Cheese and tomato tart

tender. Heat the oven to 180C /350F /gas 4.
2 Peel the marrow, cut it in half and scoop out the seeds. Blanch it in boiling water for 5 minutes, then lift it out carefully.
3 Gently fry the onion and garlic together in 40 g /1½ oz butter until soft. Add the minced beef, turn up the heat and fry it, stirring, until it is browned.
4 Turn down the heat and add the flour, cumin and turmeric. Stir to blend. Add the tomato purée and stock, then bring them to the boil. Add the sliced mushrooms and allow the mixture to simmer gently for about 10 minutes; it is ready when the mixture is quite thick.
5 Remove the pan from the heat and stir in the rice. Season to taste with salt and freshly ground black pepper.
6 Grease a large, shallow ovenproof dish. Place the marrow halves in the dish and carefully divide the stuffing between the two halves. Arrange a sliced tomato over each half and dot with the remaining 25 g /1 oz butter. Completely cover them with foil.
7 Bake the stuffed marrow in the oven for 30 minutes, then serve.

Bacon–potato bake

 1¼ hours

Serves 4
600 g /1¼ lb potatoes
15 g /½ oz butter
175 g /6 oz streaky bacon, chopped
225 g /8 oz leeks, cleaned and chopped
salt and freshly ground black pepper
25 g /1 oz plain crisps or cornflakes
50 g /2 oz Cheddar cheese, grated
30 ml /2 tbls finely chopped fresh parsley

For the tomato sauce
5 ml /1 tsp olive oil
1 garlic clove, crushed
800 g /1 lb 8 oz canned tomatoes
1.5 ml /¼ tsp celery salt
freshly ground black pepper
15 ml /1 tbls finely chopped fresh parsley

1 Heat the oven to 190C /350F /gas 5.
2 To make the tomato sauce, heat the olive oil in a saucepan, add the garlic and cook it for 30 seconds. Turn the tomatoes into a sieve over a bowl. Slit each tomato and drain off the juices. (Reserve the juices for a soup.)
3 Put the tomato flesh into the saucepan and cook it over a high heat for 12 minutes to reduce it to a thick purée. Season with celery salt and pepper, and stir in the parsley.
4 Meanwhile, peel and thinly slice the potatoes. Put them in a pan of salted water and bring them to the boil. Simmer for 5 minutes to par-boil them, then drain them.
5 Use some of the butter to grease a large gratin dish. Put the remaining butter in a saucepan and sweat the bacon until it gives off its fat. Remove the bacon with a slotted spoon. Add the chopped leeks to the saucepan and cook them in the fat until they are softened.
6 Arrange half the potatoes in the greased gratin dish and cover them with half the leeks. Season and then repeat the layers.
7 Scatter the bacon over the top and then cover it with the tomato sauce.
8 Crush the crisps or cornflakes and mix them with the cheese and parsley. Use this to cover the top of the dish. Bake it for about 30 minutes until the topping is coloured.

Cheese and tomato tart

 1¼ hours

Serves 6
275–300 g /10–11 oz made-weight shortcrust
  pastry, defrosted if frozen
350 g /12 oz firm tomatoes
30 ml /2 tbls chopped fresh herbs, including
  basil if available
6 spring onions, finely chopped
250 g /9 oz curd cheese
4 medium-sized eggs, beaten
125 g /4 oz Cheddar cheese, grated

1 Heat the oven to 200C /400F /gas 6.
2 Line a 20 cm /8 in flan tin with the pastry, then with foil and beans, and bake blind for 10 minutes. Remove the foil and beans and bake for 8 minutes more.
3 Slice the tomatoes thinly and lay the slices in the bottom of the flan case. Scatter over the herbs and spring onions.
4 Put the curd cheese into a bowl and gradually beat in the eggs. Continue to beat until the mixture is smooth. Spoon the curd mixture in an even layer over the tomatoes and then cover the top with the grated Cheddar cheese.
5 Bake the tart for 40 minutes, until the filling is set and the top is golden brown. Serve either hot or cold.

CASSEROLE TOPPINGS

Complement a tasty casserole with an equally delicious topping. I give you a wide choice, from a simple bread-and-butter topping to more unusual ones such as corn fritters and savoury crumbles, scones or custard.

When you want to make an ordinary casserole a little different — or go further if an unexpected guest arrives — try putting on a savoury topping.

Bread is one of the quickest and simplest toppings for a stew. For beef stews, coat thick slices of bread with mustard on one side and butter on the other side. Place the bread on top of the stew, mustard side down, then push it down into the stew so that the flavours mingle. Bake for 20 minutes at 200C /400F /gas 6 until a rich brown crust has formed.

Vegetables: a thick crust of mashed potato provides a perfect topping for many meat dishes, like Shepherd's soufflé (see recipe), as well as for fish dishes. You can use other vegetables, such as carrot and parsnip or swede, in the same way.

For a carrot and potato purée, use 350 g / 12 oz each of carrots and potatoes. Boil them separately in salted water until they are tender. Drain, then return them to the heat to dry off any excess moisture. Mash or sieve the vegetables, then mix them together to form a purée. Beat in 25 g /1 oz butter and about 45 ml /3 tbls milk. Check the seasoning, spoon the topping over the filling and bake for 20 minutes at 190C /375F /gas 5.

Corn fritters also make an unusual and tasty topping (see recipe).

Crumble topping is made by rubbing fat into flour in the proportions of 100 g /4 oz flour to 50 g /2 oz butter. Add seasonings and herbs that will complement the filling. For a crunchier topping, use 50 g /2 oz oats in place of 50 g /2 oz flour or add 25 g /1 oz chopped nuts to the basic mixture. Alternatively, in place of herbs, use 5 ml /1 tsp grated lemon zest or 25 g /1 oz grated cheese. Put the crumble on the filling and bake for about 30 minutes at 190C /375F /gas 5.

Dumplings are often cooked in boiling stock or water to accompany a stew or braised meat but they can be cooked on top of a stew, as in Pork hot-pot. Add extra herbs to the dumplings to suit the meat in the dish.

Forcemeat balls are made from a stuffing mixture of 100 g /4 oz fresh white breadcrumbs mixed with 50 g /2 oz suet, 15 ml / 1 tbls chopped parsley, 5 ml /1 tsp grated lemon zest, salt and freshly ground black pepper, to taste. Then 1–2 eggs are added to form a moist mixture. Formed into balls, they are usually baked in a roasting tin. They will also cook well on top of an oven-cooked casserole provided the lid is left off so that they can crisp. Cook the forcemeat balls for 20 minutes at 190C /375F /gas 5.

Vary the forcemeat mixture according to the ingredients in the casserole. Add 50 g /2 oz chopped mushrooms for beef; 50 g /2 oz chopped ham for veal; 15 ml /1 tbls chopped apple and raisins for pork.

Scones, cut into rounds or triangles, are suitable for topping oven-baked casseroles.

Make them by rubbing 50 g /2 oz butter into 225 g /8 oz self-raising flour with 5 ml /1 tsp baking powder and then mixing this with sufficient milk to make a soft dough. Roll out until 20 mm /¾ in thick, cut into shapes and bake them on top of the casserole for 20 minutes at 220C /425F /gas 7.

Make potato scones by mixing 175 g /6 oz mashed potato into the rubbed-in mixture. Make cheese scones by adding 50 g /2 oz grated cheese to the rubbed-in mixture. Alternatively, you can simply add herbs and seasonings to the basic mixture.

Gnocchi is an Italian dish made with semolina and is particularly good for topping veal or chicken stews. Bring 575 ml /1 pt milk to the boil, season with salt and pepper and add 175 g /6 oz semolina. Stir until the mixture thickens. Remove it from the heat and stir in 50 g /2 oz grated cheese and a beaten egg. Turn the mixture into a 23×23 cm /9×9 in greased tin and leave until cold. Cut into squares or triangles and arrange these over the oven-baked casserole. Sprinkle with grated cheese and bake for about 30 minutes at 190C /375F /gas 5.

Pork hot-pot

 2–2¼ hours

Serves 4
60 ml /4 tbls flour
10 ml /2 tsp mustard powder
salt and freshly ground black pepper
900 g /2 lb stewing pork, trimmed and cubed
2 medium-sized apples
45 ml /3 tbls oil
450 g /1 lb leeks, trimmed and cut into chunks
425 ml /15 fl oz stock, home-made or from a cube, or dry cider
1 bay leaf
For the dumplings
100 g /4 oz flour
5 ml /1 tsp baking powder
50 g /2 oz shredded suet
salt and freshly ground black pepper
15 ml /1 tbls freshly chopped parsley
grated zest of ½ lemon

1 Put the flour into a bowl and mix in the mustard powder, salt and pepper. Toss the meat in the seasoned flour.
2 Peel, core and chop one of the apples. Heat the oil in a large frying-pan and lightly fry the apple and leeks. Remove with a slotted spoon and set aside.
3 Add the meat to the pan and brown on all sides. Pour in the stock or cider and bring to the boil.
4 Return the fruit and vegetables to the pan. Add the bay leaf, then cover and cook gently for 1–1¼ hours until the meat is almost tender.

5 Meanwhile, make the dumplings: sieve the flour and baking powder into a bowl. Stir in the suet, salt and pepper, parsley and lemon zest. Mix with water to make a soft dough. Form into 8 balls.
6 Quarter the remaining apple, core and cut it into thick slices. Arrange the slices in the centre of the hot-pot and then arrange the dumplings around the edge. Cover and simmer for 20 minutes until the dumplings are cooked.

Mexican chicken with corn fritters

 1 hour 30 minutes

Serves 4
15 ml /1 tbls oil
15 g /½ oz butter
1 medium-sized onion, finely chopped
1.6 kg /3½ lb chicken, cut into 8 portions
10 ml /2 tsp chilli powder
400 g /14 oz canned tomatoes
1 green pepper, seeded and sliced
1 garlic clove, crushed
salt
For the corn fritters
100 g /4 oz flour
salt
1 medium-sized egg
freshly ground black pepper
150 ml /5 fl oz milk
175 g /6 oz corn kernels, drained
oil, for frying

1 Heat the oil and butter in a large frying-pan. Add the onion and cook until it is golden. Add the chicken pieces to the pan and cook until they are browned all over.
2 Sprinkle in the chilli powder and cook for 1 minute, stirring it into the pan juices. Crush the tomatoes with a fork and add them to the pan.
3 Add the green pepper and garlic and season with salt. Cover and cook for about 1 hour, or until the chicken is done; the juices should run clear when the thickest part of the flesh is pierced with a skewer.
4 Meanwhile, make the corn fritters: sift the flour and salt into a bowl. Make a well in the centre and add the egg. Season with the freshly ground black pepper and then gradually add the milk, drawing the flour in from the sides. Beat to a smooth batter, then stir in the corn kernels.
5 About 15 minutes before the chicken is done, pour oil to a depth of 5 mm /¼ in into a large frying-pan and shallow-fry the fritters: drop spoonfuls of the mixture into the oil and cook them until they are crisp and golden, turning them once.
6 Transfer the chicken pieces to a shallow serving dish, using a slotted spoon, and keep them hot. Skim off any fat from the surface of the remaining liquid. Increase the heat, and boil to reduce slightly. When the sauce has reduced and thickened, check the seasoning, then pour it over the chicken pieces. Arrange the fritters around the edge of the dish or on top of the chicken in a deeper dish. Serve immediately.

Shepherd's soufflé

 1½ hours

Serves 4
15 ml /1 tbls oil
1 medium-sized onion, finely chopped
450 g /1 lb minced beef
15 ml /1 tbls flour
100 g /4 oz mushrooms, chopped
150 ml /5 fl oz red wine
150 ml /5 fl oz beef stock, home-made or from a cube
5 ml /1 tsp Worcestershire sauce
salt
freshly ground black pepper
For the topping
450 g /1 lb potatoes, cut into equal-sized pieces
225 g /8 oz celeriac, cut into chunks
salt
freshly ground black pepper
45 ml /3 tbls milk
2 medium-sized eggs, separated

1 Heat the oil in a frying-pan. Add the onion and cook until it begins to soften. Add the mince and cook, turning, until it is browned all over. Sprinkle the flour over the meat and stir it in well.
2 Stir in the mushrooms, then the red wine, stock and Worcestershire sauce and season to taste with salt and pepper. Simmer for 25 minutes over a gentle heat.
3 Meanwhile, make the topping: cook the potatoes and celeriac separately in boiling salted water until they are soft.
4 Drain the vegetables and return them to the heat to dry off any moisture.
5 Sieve or mash the potatoes and celeriac, then combine the purées. Stir in the milk, beat in the egg yolks and adjust the seasoning. Heat the oven to 200C /400F /gas 6.
6 Whisk the egg whites until they are stiff and fold them into the mixture.
7 Turn the mince into a 1.1 L /2 pt soufflé dish and spoon the vegetable mixture over it. Bake in the oven for 30 minutes until the topping is risen and golden.

Beef bobotie

 1½ hours

Serves 6
700 g /1½ lb chuck steak
1 slice white bread, 25 mm /1 in thick
275 ml /10 fl oz milk
25 g /1 oz butter
15 ml /1 tbls olive oil
2 medium-sized onions, finely sliced
30 ml /2 tbls curry powder
30 ml /2 tbls seedless raisins
8 blanched almonds, finely chopped
15 ml /1 tbls lemon juice
2 eggs
salt
freshly ground black pepper
butter, for greasing

1 Heat the oven to 170C /325F /gas 3.
2 Trim away any gristle or fat from the meat. Cut it into small pieces and put it through the finest blade of a mincer.
3 Cut the bread into pieces, pour the milk over it and then leave to soak for 15 minutes.
4 Meanwhile, in a large heavy-based frying-pan, heat the butter and olive oil. When the foaming subsides, add the onions and sauté them over a moderate heat for 5 minutes, or until they are soft, stirring occasionally. Keep them warm.
5 Drain the unabsorbed milk from the bread into a measuring jug — there should be not less than 150 ml /5 fl oz. Reserve. Mash the soaked bread with a fork.
6 Remove the pan from the heat and stir in the curry powder, raisins, chopped almonds, lemon juice, mashed bread and minced beef. Beat in 1 egg and continue beating until the mixture is well blended. Season to taste with salt and freshly ground black pepper.
7 Butter an 850 ml /1½ pt deep pie dish and fill it with the meat.
8 Beat the remaining egg with the reserved milk. Season to taste with salt and pepper and pour it over the meat mixture.
9 Bake in the oven for 1 hour, or until the topping has set and is golden brown, and the meat is cooked. Serve at once.

● This traditional South African casserole with a custard topping is usually made with lamb and comes from Cape Malay.

Beef bobotie

IMAGINATIVE WAYS WITH MINCE

Minced meat need not be mundane; make it into meat loaves and meat balls, wrap it in pastry or serve it with a tasty sauce. This chapter has some exciting suggestions for this everyday ingredient.

Good cooks the world over favour minced meat because it is as easy to cook as it is to eat; it is economical to buy and a little can be made to go a long way. Additionally, it gives free rein to their inventiveness, for it can be shaped, stretched, seasoned and sauced in a variety of ways. For the best results, mince the meat yourself or buy your meat from a butcher who will mince it specially for you.

I have enjoyed super hamburgers and meat loaves in America, pâtés and savoury mousses in France and meat balls in almost every country of the world. Whether the origin of the dish is Moroccan or Egyptian, French or Scandinavian, Greek or Italian, it all comes down to the same basic recipe: 'take a pound of mince'.

Minced meat dishes are an ideal way of using tougher meat as the mincing process breaks up the connective tissue, making the meat quicker to cook and easier to chew. With the increased use of electric mincers and food processors, the actual preparation time for mincing your own meat is literally reduced to minutes.

What to mince?
Beef is the meat that we are most familiar with in its minced form. For 'ordinary' mince, buy lean stewing beef plus some fat; 50 g /2 oz fat to 500 g /1 lb of meat is about the right proportion. For a special dish, like my Steak tartare or Gourmet hamburgers (see recipes), you can use a more expensive cut of meat such as sirloin or fillet and omit the fat.

Of course there are all sorts of meat and poultry that can be minced; veal, pork, lamb, chicken and turkey are all suitable. A combination of meats can give a very successful flavour. You can use two or even three kinds together. Veal and pork tend to lighten both texture and taste; one of them should always dominate, in a ratio of 2:1.

How to mince
Always mince the meat just before you need to use it — prepared in advance it dries out.

Cut any skin, gristle or excess fat off the meat. Wipe it with a damp cloth or absorbent paper and cut it into small cubes that will fit your mincer or food processor.

Some recipes call for a certain texture of minced meat — hamburgers, for example, should always be coarsely ground. Your mincer will have plates with varying sized holes, so make sure that you are using the correct plates. If you are using a food processor, the length of time processing will determine the texture.
Seasoning: mixing the meat with seasonings and aromatics can be done during mincing if you are using a food processor. Personally I prefer to work the mixture with my hands, which gives me a good idea whether or not the mixture is wet enough.
Additional flavouring: the only way you

can tell if you have got the seasonings right in your mixture is to go ahead and taste it. This is not a good idea with uncooked pork, but with other fresh meat it is all right. A more laborious way of tasting it is to take about 5 ml /1 tsp of the mixture, roll it into a small ball and sauté it quickly in a little oil and butter. Incidentally, this has the added advantage that it will tell you whether or not your mixture is going to hold together when it is cooked.

Taste the cooked ball and if the flavour is not quite right, try a little tomato ketchup or tomato purée, Worcestershire sauce or Tabasco, or a little French mustard or garlic salt. If it is still not quite right, next time try sautéing some chopped onions and adding it to your mixture.
Moistening: one of the most common mistakes is to not moisten the mixture enough so the finished dish is too dry. In the majority of cases the mixture should tend towards the sloppy when raw. Do not be afraid to add a cupful of water, or stock, if the mixture feels too dry.

Shaping the mixture
Shaping patties and meat balls is again best done by hand. If you have been mixing by hand as well, wash your hands carefully, but leave them wet. Scoop up a portion of the mixture and lightly roll or pat it into the required shape. Drop it straight into the flour or egg for coating.

Serving ideas
Flavouring is very important in a minced meat dish, but almost equally important is presentation. Use your mince mixture to stuff a colourful vegetable, or spoon it over a steaming, buttery plate of golden pasta for an irresistible dish.

A meat loaf can be served with just its cooking juices, but if you add a simple tomato sauce you have a contrast of colours and flavours that makes a more pleasing combination. Serve meat balls with a sharp lemon sauce (see recipe), as the Greeks do, or a rich tomato one, like the Italians. Hamburgers are traditionally served in buns — freshly baked or toasted, slightly sweet bread often sprinkled with sesame seeds. With the hamburgers serve salads and piquant relishes. But you can also serve a really good hamburger on a plate without bread with just a salad or hot vegetables. I like to serve my Gourmet hamburger on a circle of toast spread with mustard butter — it soaks up the cooking juices without clouding the beefy flavour or adding excessive carbohydrates to your diet.

Thai minced pork

🕙 10 minutes, plus chilling,
then 7 minutes

Serves 4
225 g /8 oz minced pork
5 ml /1 tsp salt
freshly ground black pepper
1 garlic clove, finely chopped
*15 ml /1 tbls finely chopped fresh coriander
  leaves*
1 egg
15 g /½ tbls flour
50 g /2 oz canned bamboo shoots, chopped
50 g /2 oz mushrooms, finely chopped
1 egg, beaten
25–50 g /1–2 oz fresh breadcrumbs
15 ml /1 tbls olive oil
15 g /½ oz butter
spring onion, to garnish

1 In a large bowl, combine the minced pork, salt, freshly ground black pepper, chopped garlic, the chopped coriander leaves, egg, flour, canned bamboo shoots and the finely chopped mushrooms. Mix them together well and adjust the seasoning.
2 With wet hands, shape the mixture into 8 small balls. Coat the balls in the beaten egg and roll them in the breadcrumbs. Chill the balls for at least 30 minutes.
3 Heat the oil and butter in a large frying-pan and sauté the meat balls for 5 minutes or until the pork is no longer pink. Garnish with the spring onion and serve immediately, supplying cocktail sticks for spearing the meat balls.

Steak tartare

This raw beef dish is the ultimate in minced meat recipes.

 30 minutes

Serves 1
225 g /8 oz fillet or sirloin steak
salt
freshly ground black pepper
1 egg yolk
30 ml /2 tbls finely chopped onion
30 ml /2 tbls chopped capers
a few drops of Tabasco sauce

1 Wipe the steak with a damp cloth or absorbent paper, cut it into even-sized pieces. Put the steak through the coarse blade of a mincer, or work it briefly in a food processor. Season to taste with salt and freshly ground black pepper.
2 On an individual serving plate, shape the steak into a round. Make a dip in the centre with the back of a spoon and place the egg yolk in the depression.
3 In a small bowl mix together the finely chopped onion and capers, a few drops of Tabasco sauce and salt and freshly ground black pepper to taste.
4 Spoon the onion and caper mixture onto the serving plate beside the steak and serve them immediately.

Fresh ingredients for minced meat dishes

Spinach-wrapped terrine

 3 hours

Serves 4

25 g /1 oz butter
½ Spanish onion, finely chopped
500 g /1 lb minced lamb
4 slices bread, coarsely chopped
150 ml /5 fl oz milk
5 ml /1 tsp tomato purée
45 ml /3 tbls meat glaze (see note below)
salt and freshly ground black pepper
150 g /5 oz whole spinach leaves
olive oil, for greasing

For the sauce

25 g /1 oz butter
45 ml /3 tbls flour
275 ml /10 fl oz milk
salt and freshly ground black pepper
1 egg, beaten
25 g /1 oz Gruyère cheese, grated

1 Heat the oven to 180C /350F /gas 4.
2 Make the sauce. In a saucepan melt the butter, add the flour and cook for 1–2 minutes, stirring constantly. Blend in the milk and bring to the boil, still stirring. Cook the sauce over a gentle heat for 15 minutes or until it is smooth and thickened. Season to taste with salt and freshly ground black pepper. Lower the heat and stir in the beaten egg. Cook for 2–3 minutes, but do not allow it to boil. Remove it from the heat and stir in the grated Gruyère cheese. Set aside.
3 In a frying-pan, melt the butter and cook the onion until brown. Add the lamb and cook until brown. Pour off any fat.
4 Meanwhile put the bread in a bowl, add the milk, and leave it to soak.
5 Add the tomato purée and meat glaze to the lamb and onion mixture and season to taste. Squeeze the milk from the bread and add it to the lamb mixture.
6 Carefully remove the stalks from the spinach leaves, trying to keep the leaves whole. Wash them thoroughly and then blanch them in boiling water for 1 minute. Drain and refresh them under cold running

Thai minced pork — ideal for handing round with drinks at a party

water, then lay them gently on a clean tea-towel to dry.
7 Brush a 700 ml /1¼ pt loaf tin with oil and line the tin with the spinach leaves. Leave enough leaves hanging over the edge of the tin to cover the finished terrine.
8 Place a thin layer of lamb mixture on the base of the tin and cover it with a layer of sauce. Repeat until the mince and sauce are used up — finishing with a layer of lamb. Now fold the spinach leaves over the top of the terrine.
9 Stand the loaf tin in a roasting tin and pour in boiling water to a depth of 25 mm /1 in. Bake the terrine in the oven for 45 minutes or until it is firm.
10 Pour off any excess liquid from the tin and turn out the terrine. Serve immediately.

● To make the meat glaze, put 425 g /15 oz good quality canned consommé in a saucepan and then boil it fast for 20 minutes until it is reduced to 45 ml /3 tbls of syrupy glaze.

Minced turkey in spicy basil sauce

 1 hour 20 minutes

Serves 4
3 medium-sized eggs
350 g /12 oz cooked turkey meat, minced
5 ml /1 tsp coriander seeds, crushed
2.5 ml /½ tsp blades of mace, crushed
salt
freshly ground black pepper
15 ml /1 tbls olive oil (optional)
fresh white breadcrumbs, for coating
50 g /2 oz butter
For the sauce
30 ml /2 tbls olive oil
1 onion, very finely chopped
1 garlic clove, finely chopped
1 small green chilli, seeded and chopped
400 g /14 oz canned tomatoes
45 ml /3 tbls chopped fresh basil
salt
freshly ground black pepper

1 In a large bowl, beat 2 of the eggs. Add the minced turkey and beat well. Add the coriander seeds, mace and salt and pepper to taste and mix well. If the mixture seems too dry, add the olive oil.
2 Beat the remaining egg in a shallow bowl and place the breadcrumbs on a plate.
3 Form the turkey mixture into 8 rounds about 5 cm /2 in in diameter and 6–12 mm / ¼–½ in thick. Dip each one in the egg and then into the breadcrumbs, making sure each is well coated. Place them on a plate in the refrigerator to firm up while you make the basil sauce.
4 To make the sauce, heat the oil in a large saucepan over a low heat. Add the onion, garlic and chilli and cook gently until the onion is very soft.
5 Purée the tomatoes and basil in a blender. Add them to the saucepan and season with salt and freshly ground black pepper. Simmer gently for 10 minutes or until the sauce is thick.
6 Shortly before the sauce is done, melt the butter in a large frying-pan and add the turkey rounds, 4 at a time, so that they sit comfortably side by side. Fry for 3–4 minutes each side, until crispy and golden. Remove with a slotted spoon and keep warm while you fry the remaining ones.
7 Place the turkey rounds on a large, warmed serving platter, pour the sauce over them and serve at once.

Spicy pork tamales

 1 hour 30 minutes

Serves 4 as a main course
12 corn husks (optional)
For the pancakes
50 g /2 oz vegetable fat or lard
175 g /6 oz polenta
5 ml /1 tsp baking powder
5 ml /1 tsp salt

For the filling
175 g /6 oz lean minced pork
1 small onion, very finely chopped
1 dried red chilli, seeded and finely chopped
1 tomato, blanched, skinned, seeded and chopped
10 ml /2 tsp freshly chopped coriander leaves or mint leaves
a pinch of salt

1 Soak the corn husks, if you are going to use them, in very hot water for about 10 minutes, to make them supple, then drain and pat them dry with absorbent paper. Alternatively, you can use rectangles of foil, 23 × 10 cm /9 × 4 in.
2 To make the pancakes, cream the fat until it is light and fluffy. Sift together the polenta, baking powder and salt. Alternately beat in small amounts of the corn mixture and about 300 ml /10 fl oz water into the fat, until it becomes a smooth but moist dough.
3 Arrange the corn husks or foil on a work surface and divide the dough among them, spreading it out in the centre of each to make a 9 cm /3½ in square.
4 Mix together the filling ingredients to form a moist paste. Divide the filling among the containers of dough, spooning it into the centre. Fold the sides of the husk or foil into the centre so that the dough forms a 'tube' with a centre join. Fold over the top and ends of the wrapping, to enclose the parcels completely. Tie them with fine string.
5 Place the parcels on a steaming rack or in a colander that fits inside a saucepan. Cover this with foil and then with the lid, and steam over boiling water for 50 minutes.
6 Untie the strings and then serve the tamales immediately.

Veal and apple patties with fresh sage

 40 minutes, plus chilling

Serves 6
700 g /1½ lb lean minced veal
2 dessert apples, peeled, cored and finely chopped
½ Spanish onion, finely chopped
1 egg, beaten
salt and freshly ground black pepper
60 ml /4 tbls flour
25 g /1 oz butter
30 ml /2 tbls olive oil
20 fresh sage leaves
125 ml /8 tbls dry white wine
bouquet of sage, to garnish (optional)

1 In a bowl, combine the veal, the apples and the onion. Stir in the beaten egg to bind and season with salt and pepper.
2 With wet hands, shape the mixture into 6 even-sized patties and lay them on a tray lined with cling film. Refrigerate for 30 minutes.
3 Sprinkle the flour onto a plate and toss each patty to coat it.
4 In a frying-pan large enough to take the veal in a single layer, heat the butter and olive oil. When the foaming subsides, lay the patties side by side in the hot fat. Place 8 sage leaves between the patties and sauté over a moderate heat for 4 minutes; then turn the patties over and continue to sauté until they are cooked through.
5 Remove the patties with a slotted spoon. Drain on absorbent paper and arrange on a heated serving dish. Keep hot.
6 Pour the dry white wine into the juices remaining in the pan. Bring to the boil, scraping the pan with a wooden spoon to mix in any sediment. Boil until the sauce has reduced by ⅓ and strain over the veal patties. Arrange 2 fresh sage leaves on top of each and serve immediately, garnished with a bouquet of sage, if wished.

● Serve these tasty patties with a fresh green salad and a mound of crisp, golden French-fried potatoes.

Veal and apple patties with fresh sage

Moroccan cigars

Serve these spiced minced chicken 'cigars' made with flaky filo pastry as a snack or as finger food with drinks. You will find them absolutely irresistible.

 1¾ hours

Makes 12
25 g /1 oz butter
15 ml /1 tbls olive oil
1 Spanish onion, finely chopped
700 g /1½ lb raw chicken, minced (the meat from 5 leg portions)
5 ml /1 tsp ground coriander
2.5 ml /½ tsp ground cumin
1.5 ml /¼ tsp ground ginger
2.5 ml /½ tsp turmeric
5 ml /1 tsp salt
freshly ground black pepper
15 ml /1 tbls flour
150 ml /5 fl oz chicken stock, home-made or from a cube
6 sheets filo pastry, 48×25 cm /19×10 in
75–125 g /3–4 oz butter, melted

1 Heat the oven to 220C /425F /gas 7.
2 Heat 15 g /½ oz butter and the olive oil in a frying-pan and sauté the finely chopped onion for 1–2 minutes until softened. Add the minced chicken and cook for 10–15 minutes, until cooked. Add the ground coriander, cumin, ginger, turmeric, salt and freshly ground black pepper and stir well.
3 Meanwhile, melt the remaining butter and stir in the flour to form a roux. Cook for 1–2 minutes and add the chicken stock. Bring to the boil and cook for 5 minutes or until it has thickened. Add this sauce to the minced chicken. Allow it to cool slightly.
4 Fold a sheet of filo pastry in three lengthways and cut it in half to make two 12.5 cm / 5 in lengths. Brush the top surface of the folded pastry with melted butter and place 45 ml /3 tbls of the chicken mixture down the centre. Roll up the cigar, trimming the ends and wrapping them in as you roll. Brush well with butter and place on a baking tray. Repeat with the remaining pastry and chicken mixture to make 12 cigars.
5 Cook in the oven for 10–12 minutes. Serve immediately.

Gourmet hamburgers

Gourmet hamburgers

Serve these hamburgers with fried onion rings, tomato wedges and a green salad.

 30 minutes

Serves 4
900 g /2 lb lean roasting beef, such as topside
salt and freshly ground black pepper
oil, for greasing
4 slices bread, 15 mm /½ in thick
50 g /2 oz butter, softened
10 ml /2 tsp Dijon mustard

1 Blot the meat with absorbent paper, cut into even-sized pieces. Heat the grill to high.
2 Put the beef through the coarse blade of the mincer, or process it in a food processor.
3 Season with salt and freshly ground black pepper. Divide the minced meat into four and shape each portion into a burger 4 cm /1½ in thick. Avoid handling the meat too much; the burgers do not need to be tightly packed as they are not turned during cooking.
4 Brush the grill grid with oil and place the burgers on it. Cook 7.5 cm /3 in from the heat for 8 minutes, on one side only.

Meat loaf 'in shirtsleeves'

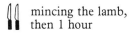 1¼ hours, cooling,
then 1 hour

Serves 4–6
15 g /½ oz butter, plus extra for greasing
1 Spanish onion, very finely chopped
3 slices stale white bread
75–150 ml /3–5 fl oz beef stock, home-made
  or from a cube
225 g /8 oz lean minced beef
225 g /8 oz lean minced pork
30 ml /2 tbls finely chopped fresh parsley
5 ml /1 tsp Worcestershire sauce
a dash of Tabasco sauce or cayenne pepper
salt and freshly ground black pepper
225 g /8 oz made-weight puff pastry, defrosted
  if necessary
60 ml /4 tbls French mustard
beaten egg, to glaze
parsley sprigs, to garnish

1 Heat the oven to 220C /425F /gas 7.
2 Melt the butter in a heavy frying-pan and sauté the onion slowly until soft.
3 Trim the bread of crusts. Soak the slices in a little beef stock or water; then squeeze out as much moisture as possible.
4 In a large bowl, combine the sautéed onion and soaked bread with the minced beef and pork, chopped parsley and Worcestershire sauce, and Tabasco or cayenne to taste. Mix until smoothly blended, adding generous amounts of salt and black pepper.
5 Grease an 850 ml /1½ pt loaf tin with butter. Firmly pack the meat mixture into it and level off the top. Cover it with foil.
6 Bake the meat loaf for 45 minutes. Next, remove it from the oven and leave to become quite cold before putting it 'in shirtsleeves'.
7 When ready to proceed, heat the oven to 200C /400F /gas 6.
8 Roll out the puff pastry into a 30 cm /12 in square. Turn the meat loaf out of its tin; scrape off any excess fat and spread the loaf liberally with French mustard.
9 Set the meat loaf in the centre of the pastry square and wrap it up like a parcel. Brush the seams lightly with water; seal them tightly and trim away the excess pastry. Use the scraps to make a lattice of strips over the top. Brush the pastry with beaten egg and cut small vents on top to allow steam to escape.
10 Transfer the pastry-wrapped meat loaf to an ungreased baking sheet and bake for 30 minutes, or until the pastry is well puffed, crisp and golden. Serve hot, cut in thick slices, garnished with parsley.

● Serve the meat loaf with a fresh tomato sauce: blanch and skin 1 kg /2 lb tomatoes, and remove their seeds and juice. Chop the flesh into 5–10 mm /¼–½ in dice. In a pan, sauté 60 ml /4 tbls finely chopped onion in 30 ml /2 tbls olive oil until the onion is soft. Add the diced tomato, plus two finely chopped garlic cloves and a generous pinch each of dried oregano and caster sugar. Season. Simmer for 10–15 minutes. Adjust the seasoning, then stir in 30 ml /2 tbls finely chopped fresh parsley and serve.

5 Meanwhile, toast the bread and cut a 10 cm /4 in circle from each slice. Blend the butter and mustard together and spread the mixture on the toast.
6 Place a hamburger on each slice of toast and serve immediately.

Greek meat balls with lemon sauce

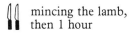 mincing the lamb,
then 1 hour

Serves 4
500 g /1 lb minced lamb
½ onion, finely chopped
90 ml /6 tbls long-grain rice
60 ml /4 tbls chopped fresh parsley
10 ml /2 tsp salt
freshly ground black pepper
60 ml /4 tbls iced water
boiled rice, to serve
For the lemon sauce
2 egg yolks
30 ml /2 tbls lemon juice
300 ml /10 fl oz chicken stock, home-made or
  from a cube
salt and freshly ground black pepper

Meat loaf 'in shirtsleeves'

1 In a large mixing bowl, combine the minced lamb, chopped onion, rice, half the chopped parsley, the salt, and a generous amount of freshly ground black pepper. Add the iced water and mix well. Adjust the seasoning, if necessary.
2 With wet hands, shape the mixture into meat balls.
3 Bring a large pan of salted water to the boil and drop in the meat balls one by one. Bring the water back to the boil, then reduce the heat so that the water just simmers and cook the meat balls for 45 minutes.
4 Meanwhile, make the lemon sauce. In a small bowl, beat together the egg yolks and lemon juice. Heat the stock to boiling and whisk a little into the egg yolk mixture. Pour this mixture into the saucepan of stock, place it over a low heat and cook, stirring constantly, for 3 minutes or until the sauce is slightly thickened. Do not let it boil or it will curdle. Adjust the seasoning.
5 When the meat balls are cooked, remove them from the bouillon with a slotted spoon and arrange them on a heated serving dish. Pour the lemon sauce over them and sprinkle the top with the remaining chopped parsley. Serve them with plain boiled rice.

USING UP LEFT-OVER CHICKEN

You can make a whole range of attractive dishes from left-over chicken. Try some of these inventive ideas, ranging from easy-to-prepare snacks to more elaborate creations.

The most succulent chicken meat comes from whole birds cooked by pot-roasting or simmering. If you simmer the chicken, you also have the bonus of well-flavoured stock which can be used for sauces and soups.

Simmered chicken is very simple to prepare and uses a minimum of fuel. Choose a pan with a tightly fitting lid, and one into which the bird will fit fairly closely. Fill the pan with water to a depth of 4 cm /1½ in, add the washed giblets (excluding the liver), several small onions, chunky pieces of carrot and celery, a bay leaf, a strip of lemon peel, 6 peppercorns and 5 ml /1 tsp salt.

Bring the water to simmering point and add the washed chicken. Cover it and simmer for 1–1¼ hours for a 1.5–2 kg /3¼–4½ lb bird. Remove the chicken from the pan and strain the stock, reserving the vegetables. Make a sauce with some of the strained stock and serve it with the chicken and vegetables. Remember to refrigerate the stock and the left-over chicken as soon as they are cold. If it is not convenient to use them within 3 days, allow them to cool and then freeze them until they are needed.

The following four recipes use cooked chicken in very different ways. The quantities are not criticial so do not worry if you have a little more chicken than the recipe states. In general, use larger amounts of left-over chicken for a substantial pie, salad or jellied chicken dish.

Chicken and tuna-stuffed tomatoes are ideal for lunch, served with a salad and hot crusty French bread. For a stylish dish, try Timbales of chicken served with a rich Madeira sauce, or Chicken pancakes amandine, with a delicious chicken, sherry and mushroom filling. Chicken croûtes are fairly quick to make for a lovely supper-time treat.

Chicken and tuna-stuffed tomatoes

🍴 20 minutes

Serves 4
8 medium-sized firm, ripe tomatoes
salt
75 g /3 oz cooked chicken, finely chopped
100 g /3½ oz canned tuna fish in oil
3 canned anchovy fillets, drained
75 ml /5 tbls thick mayonnaise
10 ml /2 tsp lemon juice
freshly ground black pepper
2 hard-boiled eggs
crisp lettuce leaves, to garnish

1 Cut a thin slice from the top of each tomato. Scoop out the flesh with a teaspoon and reserve it for a soup or sauce. Sprinkle the inside of the tomato cases with a little salt

and then leave them upside down to drain.
2 Press the tuna fish with its oil and the anchovy fillets through a sieve into a bowl, then stir in the mayonnaise, lemon juice and a sprinkling of pepper. Alternatively, combine these ingredients in an electric blender.
3 Cut 4 slices from the centre of each hard-boiled egg and reserve them for garnishing. Chop the remainder. Stir the chopped egg and the chicken into the tuna mayonnaise and check the seasoning.
4 Fill the tomato cases with the mixture, top them with a slice of egg and arrange them on a bed of lettuce leaves.

Timbales of chicken

🍴🍴🍴 cooking the chicken,
then 1 hour

Serves 8
25 g /1 oz butter, plus extra for greasing
350 g /12 oz cooked, boned chicken
225 g /8 oz cooked ham
150 g /5 oz button mushrooms, finely chopped
¼ Spanish onion, finely chopped
salt and freshly ground black pepper
1 egg, beaten
1 small green pepper, diced
For the cheese sauce
15 g /½ oz butter
15 ml /1 tbls flour
150 ml /5 fl oz milk
30 ml /2 tbls Gruyère cheese, freshly grated
For the Maderia sauce
25 g /1 oz butter
30 ml /2 tbls flour
125 ml /4 fl oz milk
150 ml /5 fl oz thick cream
freshly grated nutmeg
15 ml /1 tbls Madeira

1 Heat the oven to 170C /375F /gas 3. Cut and butter greaseproof paper circles to fit the bottom of 8 × 150 ml /5 fl oz dariole moulds. Butter the moulds and then line them with the buttered paper circles. Put the cooked chicken and ham through the finest blade of the mincer.
2 In a small saucepan, melt 25 g /1 oz butter. Sauté the finely chopped mushrooms and onion over a moderate heat for 7–10 minutes, or until the onion is soft, stirring occasionally. Leave them to cool.
3 Meanwhile, make the cheese sauce. In a saucepan, melt the butter and stir in the flour to blend. Cook, stirring, over a low heat for 2–3 minutes, to make a pale roux. Gradually pour in the milk, stirring vigorously with a wire whisk to prevent lumps forming. Simmer for 2–3 minutes, or until it is thickened, stirring occasionally. Season to taste with salt and freshly ground black pepper. Stir in the cheese.
4 Beat the cheese sauce and mushroom

mixture into the minced meat and season to taste with salt and freshly ground black pepper. Beat in the egg to bind it. Spoon the mixture into the moulds, smoothing the tops with the back of the spoon. Cover them with foil and place them in a small roasting tin. Add boiling water to come 25 mm /1 in up the side of the moulds and bake them for 30 minutes, or until they are set. Remove the roasting tin from the oven. Cover the moulds with foil and keep them warm.
5 Meanwhile, make the Madeira sauce. In a small saucepan, melt the butter. Stir in the flour to blend and cook, stirring, over a low heat for 2–3 minutes to make a pale roux. Gradually pour in the milk and thick cream, stirring vigorously with a wire whisk to prevent lumps forming. Simmer for 2–3 minutes until the mixture is thickened, stirring occasionally. Season with a little nutmeg, salt and freshly ground black pepper to taste. Stir in the Madeira.
6 Unmould the timbales onto a hot serving

Timbales of chicken

platter. Remove the paper, then pour a little sauce over each timbale. Spoon the diced green pepper into the centre of the dish, then serve immediately.

Chicken croûtes

Tasty chicken in a cheese sauce is delicious when piled on top of quickly-prepared crisp bread croûtes.

 30 minutes

Serves 4
50 g /2 oz butter
25 g /1 oz flour
250 ml /9 fl oz chicken stock, home-made or
  from a cube
30 ml /2 tbls thin cream or milk
100 g /4 oz cooked chicken, chopped
50 g /2 oz Cheddar cheese, grated
50 g /2 oz mild garlic sausage, or ham,
  finely chopped
salt
freshly ground black pepper
4 large slices bread with crusts removed
a little chopped fresh parsley, to garnish

1 Melt 25 g /1 oz of the butter in a small saucepan. Add the flour and stir over a low heat for 1 minute. Gradually stir in the stock, cream or milk and bring to the boil, stirring briskly. Simmer until the sauce is thick and smooth.
2 Add the chicken, cheese, two-thirds of the garlic sausage or ham and salt and freshly ground black pepper to taste. Heat the mixture, stirring continuously.
3 Meanwhile, toast the bread slices on one side. Turn them over and spread them with the remaining butter. Toast them under a low heat until they are crisp and golden.
4 Pile the chicken mixture on top of the toast. Garnish with the remaining garlic sausage or ham, mixed with the chopped parsley. Serve immediately, so that the toast does not become soft.

● The tasty chicken mixture in this recipe also makes an excellent filling for shortcrust pastry tartlets or puff pastry bouchée or vol-au-vent cases. Cook the tartlets or cases first, then fill them with the hot mixture.
● The garlic sausage or ham may be replaced by 100 g /4 oz button mushrooms or a mixture of mushrooms and onions, sliced, gently fried in butter and drained.

Chicken pancakes amandine

These pancakes are stuffed with a chicken filling and topped with almonds.

🍴 1 hour

Serves 4
100 g /4 oz flour
1.5 ml /¼ tsp salt
2 medium-sized eggs
250 ml /8 fl oz milk
15 ml /1 tbls melted butter or oil
a little oil, for greasing
For the filling
25 g /1 oz butter
25 g /1 oz flour
250 ml /10 fl oz chicken stock, home-made or
  from a cube
30 ml /2 tbls medium sherry
175 g /6 oz cooked chicken, chopped
212 g /7½ oz canned button mushrooms,
  drained and sliced
salt and freshly ground black pepper
For the topping
25 g /1 oz butter
15 ml /1 tbls oil
25 g /1 oz flaked almonds
5 ml /1 tsp lemon juice
sprigs of parsley, to garnish

1 Sift the flour and salt into a bowl and make a well in the centre. Put the eggs and half the milk into the well and mix them with a wooden spoon or wire whisk, gradually drawing in the flour and beating briskly to form a smooth, thick batter.
2 Beat in the remaining milk and leave the mixture, covered, until it is required. Just before using it, beat in the butter or oil.
3 To cook the pancakes, grease the base of an 18 cm /7 in frying-pan with about 2.5 ml / ½ tsp oil and heat until the pan and oil are thoroughly hot. Pour in about 30 ml /2 tbls of the batter and immediately swirl it around to coat the base of the pan thinly.
4 Cook for about 1 minute, until the pancake has set and is lightly browned. Next, turn it over and cook the other side for a few seconds. Turn it out onto a flat surface and leave it to cool. Repeat with the remaining batter to make 8 or 9 pancakes. Heat the oven to 200C /400F /gas 6.
5 For the filling, melt the butter in a saucepan, stir in the flour and cook for 1 minute. Beat in the stock and heat, stirring, to form a sauce. Simmer it for several minutes.
6 Stir in the sherry, chicken, mushrooms and salt and pepper to taste.
7 Arrange about 30 ml /2 tbls of the filling along the centre of each pancake. Roll them up and arrange them side by side in a single layer in a buttered, shallow ovenproof dish. Cover it with foil and cook the pancakes in the oven for 25 minutes, until they are hot.
8 Meanwhile, to make the topping, heat the butter and oil in a frying-pan and gently fry the almonds until they are golden, stirring frequently. Add the lemon juice to the pan. Stir, scatter the almonds over the hot pancakes, and serve, garnished with parsley.

ECONOMICAL DESSERTS

These lovely desserts are perfect if you're keeping an eye on costs: they make the best use of basic ingredients and seasonal fruits to produce a variety of economical sweets that all the family will love.

A pudding need not be an expensive end to a meal — and it need not be time-consuming to prepare either. With a little imagination, economical puddings can easily be made by combining basic store-cupboard ingredients — such as eggs and flour — with cheap seasonal fruit, dried fruit, nuts, grains and milk or yoghurt instead of cream.

Fruit: when choosing fruit, steer clear of expensive imported items. Make the most of home-grown fruit when it is in season, such as apples, rhubarb and gooseberries (see recipes). If you stew or bottle fruit it will always be available when you need it.

Dried fruit is not as extravagant as it may seem — prunes and apricots, once soaked and cooked, stretch a long way and have a good flavour (see recipe for Prune and orange mousse). Sultanas, raisins, currants and dates add sweetness and you will not need to use many of them.

Nuts: add chopped nuts, either as decoration or as part of the actual pudding, to give a contrasting texture and flavour.

Grains: Creamy milk puddings give good nutritional value and, when made properly, will appeal to both children and adults. Grains are cheap to buy, they store well and go a long way. Make rice, semolina and tapioca puddings mixed with dried fruit for added interest.

Leftovers can be used as excellent bases for economical puddings. Try using up sponge cake in a trifle; egg whites whisked to make meringue give a special touch to desserts such as Rhubarb amber and Queen of puddings (see recipes). Bread is a thrifty base for many puddings, both baked and steamed, using spices and dried fruit. Try my Chocolate bread pudding for a substantial dessert. Broken biscuits can be finely crushed and then used to make a tasty topping for a creamy cold sweet (see recipe for Ginger peach sundae); or mix them with melted butter to line a flan case instead of using a pastry base.

Prune and orange mousse

overnight soaking the prunes, 20 minutes, plus chilling

Serves 6
225 g /8 oz prunes, soaked overnight in water to cover
50 g /2 oz Demerara sugar
a strip of lemon zest
grated zest and juice of one orange
15 g /½ oz gelatine
150 ml /5 fl oz whipping cream
1 medium-sized egg white
To garnish
thin strips of orange zest

1 Cover the soaked prunes with water and poach them with the sugar and lemon zest until just tender. Cool; lift out the prunes and stone them. Discard the zest and stones. Make up the juice to 150 ml /5 fl oz with water.
2 Put the prune flesh and syrup, together with 5 ml /1 tsp orange zest and the orange juice, into a blender and purée, allowing some flecks of prune to remain.
3 Put the gelatine in a pan with 30 ml /2 tbls water. Leave to soak for 2 minutes, then put it over a gentle heat to dissolve. Stir it into the prune purée.
4 Whip the cream lightly, then stir it into the prune purée.
5 Whisk the egg white until stiff. Carefully fold it into the prune mixture, turn it into a wetted 1 L /2 pt jelly mould and leave it to set in the refrigerator for about 2 hours.
6 To turn out the mousse, dip the jelly mould in a bowl of hot water for 30 seconds. Gently press the edge of the mousse away from the mould with your finger, then invert the mould onto a plate to turn it out. Garnish the mousse with thin strips of orange zest.

Crêpes with plum sauce

30 minutes

Serves 4–6
100 g /4 oz flour
1.5 ml /¼ tsp salt
1 medium-sized egg, beaten
250 ml /10 fl oz milk
butter, for frying
550 g /1 lb 4 oz canned Victoria plums
50 g /2 oz caster sugar
finely grated zest and juice of half a lemon
50 g /2 oz butter, melted
icing sugar, for dusting

1 Sift the flour and salt into a large bowl. Pour in the beaten egg, then slowly pour half the milk into the flour, gradually working the flour into the milk with a wooden spoon. Beat well until it becomes free of lumps. Add the remainder of the milk, beating until the batter is bubbly and has the consistency of thin cream.
2 To make the crêpes, add just enough butter to gloss a small frying-pan and heat over a fairly high heat. Pour in enough batter to flow in a thin film over the base, tilting the pan to spread it around. Cook the crêpe for 1 minute.
3 Turn over the crêpe and cook it until the second side is lightly browned. Turn it onto a plate. To keep the crêpes hot, pile them between two plates over a pan of simmering water. Repeat until all the batter is used up (it should make about 12 crêpes).

4 To make the plum sauce, remove the stones from the plums, then blend or sieve them with their juice to make a purée. Place the plum purée in a saucepan with the sugar, lemon zest and lemon juice; heat them all together gently.
5 Spread each crêpe with melted butter, then sprinkle with icing sugar. Roll up the crêpes and serve the sauce separately.

Ginger peach sundae

chilling the evaporated milk, then 10 minutes

Serves 4
100 g /4 oz ginger biscuits, finely crushed
400 g /14 oz canned peach slices, drained
175 ml /6 fl oz canned evaporated milk, well chilled
30 ml /2 tbls icing sugar, sieved

1 Crush the biscuits in a bag with a rolling pin, or in a blender. Chop the peaches.

2 Whisk the evaporated milk with an electric whisk until it resembles whipped cream. Fold in the sieved icing sugar.

3 Divide half of the peaches among four glasses. Cover with half of the biscuit crumbs.

4 Spoon the whisked evaporated milk into the four glasses. Add the rest of the peaches, then top with the remaining biscuit crumbs.

Rhubarb amber

The pastry case and filling can be made and stored (separately) in advance.

65 minutes, including chilling the pastry case, then 30 minutes

Serves 4–6
175 g /6 oz flour
a pinch of salt
7.5 ml /1½ tsp caster sugar
115 g /4½ oz butter
1 medium-sized egg yolk
2.5 ml /½ tsp iced water

For the filling and topping
450 g /1 lb rhubarb, stewed with sugar, drained and puréed
5 ml /1 tsp grated lemon zest
25 g /1 oz butter, melted
2 medium-sized eggs, separated
a pinch of salt
50 g /2 oz caster sugar

1 Make the pastry: sieve the flour and salt into a large mixing bowl and stir in the sugar. Using a chilled palette knife, or a pastry cutter, cut the butter into the flour until the mixture resembles fine breadcrumbs. Make a well in the centre.

2 Beat together the egg yolk and water and pour this into the well. With the palette knife, draw the dry ingredients into the egg. With your fingertips, gather the mixture together to make a soft dough. Turn it onto a lightly-floured surface and knead it briefly until smooth. Wrap it in cling film and leave it in the refrigerator to rest for 30 minutes.

3 Heat the oven to 200C /400F /gas 6. Allow the dough to soften for a few minutes at room temperature. Use the dough to line a 20 cm /8 in diameter fluted flan tin, gently pressing it over the base and up the sides. Trim the edges of the pastry and leave it to chill in the refrigerator for 10 minutes.

4 Line the pastry case with foil and dried beans and bake blind for 10 minutes; remove the foil and beans and return the pastry case to the oven for 5 minutes more. Remove it from the oven.

5 Reduce the oven temperature to 180C /350F /gas 4. Make the rhubarb filling: combine the rhubarb purée, lemon zest, melted butter and egg yolks and beat them with a wooden spoon until smoothly blended. Pour the filling into the pastry case and bake it for 15 minutes until it is just set.

6 Place the egg whites in a clean, dry bowl, add the salt and whisk until stiff. Whisk in half the caster sugar; reserve 5 ml /1 tsp sugar, then fold in the remainder.

7 Pile the meringue over the filling, taking it right to the edges and making sure it meets the pastry rim. Sprinkle the reserved 5 ml /1 tsp caster sugar over the top of the meringue. To serve warm: bake for a further 10 minutes until the meringue is lightly browned. To serve cold, bake at 150C /300F /gas 2 for 20–30 minutes, so the meringue topping is firmer and dryer.

Apple dumplings

1 hour

Serves 4
225 g /8 oz flour
2.5 ml /½ tsp salt
50 g /2 oz margarine
50 g /2 oz lard
4 large tart apples, peeled and cored
50 g /2 oz brown sugar
zest of ½ lemon
25 g /1 oz sultanas
a good pinch of cinnamon
milk, to glaze
caster sugar, for dusting

1 Sift the flour into a bowl with the salt and rub in the fats until the mixture resembles fine breadcrumbs. Add about 45 ml /3 tbls cold water to make a dough, then knead it lightly on a floured surface. Chill it for 30 minutes before using it. Heat the oven to 200C /400F /gas 6.

2 Thinly roll out the pastry into a square. Cut it into four equal squares, reserving the trimmings. Place an apple in the centre of each square. Mix together the brown sugar, lemon zest, sultanas and cinnamon and use this to fill the centre of each apple.

3 Dampen the edges of the pastry and bring the edges up, pinching them together and completely enclosing the apple.

4 Place the apples on a greased baking tray. Cut 16 pastry leaves from the trimmings, moisten with water and attach 4 leaves to each apple.

5 Brush the dumplings with milk and dust with caster sugar. Bake for 30 minutes and then serve hot.

Crêpes with plum sauce, and Apple dumplings

Chocolate bread pudding

 about 2 hours

Serves 6–8

50 g /2 oz butter, plus extra for greasing
75 g /3 oz plain chocolate
150 ml /5 fl oz milk
60 ml /4 tbls caster sugar
2 eggs, separated
150 g /5 oz fresh white breadcrumbs
1.5 ml /¼ tsp ground cinnamon
2.5 ml /½ tsp vanilla essence

1 Generously butter an 850 ml /1½ pt pudding bowl.
2 Break the chocolate into the top pan of a double boiler and add 50 g /2 oz butter. Heat over simmering water, stirring with a wooden spoon until the chocolate has melted. Pour in the milk and stir to blend. Remove the mixture from the heat.
3 Stir in the caster sugar, then the egg yolks and the breadcrumbs. Flavour the mixture with ground cinnamon and vanilla essence and mix well.
4 In a clean, dry bowl, whisk the egg whites to stiff peaks. Gently fold this into the chocolate breadcrumb mixture with a large metal spoon, working quickly and lightly.
5 Pour the pudding into the prepared bowl. Cover it with a double thickness of foil and tie it with string.
6 Place the bowl in the top of a steamer. Steam for 1½ hours over boiling water, until the chocolate bread pudding is well risen and firm to the touch, adding more boiling water as necessary.
7 Remove the pudding bowl from the steamer. Run a knife around the edge of the pudding, between the bowl and the pudding. Turn the pudding out onto a heated serving platter and serve immediately.

● Serve the Chocolate bread pudding with 575 ml /1 pt custard, flavoured with 30 ml / 2 tbls Grand Marnier, if wished.

Gooseberry pie

 making the pastry, then 2 hours

Serves 4–6

900 g /2 lb hard green gooseberries
45 ml /3 tbls soft dark brown sugar
20 ml /4 tsp cornflour
flour, for rolling
250 g /8 oz made-weight puff pastry,
  defrosted if frozen
1 egg, lightly beaten
15 ml /1 tbls caster sugar
300 ml /10 fl oz thick cream, to serve

1 Wash the gooseberries in a colander under cold running water. Next, top and tail them and put them in a 1.1 L /2 pt pie dish. Add the sugar and toss the gooseberries.
2 In a small bowl, blend the cornflour with 15 ml /1 tbls cold water. Sprinkle it over the

gooseberries and toss them again until they are well mixed.
3 On a floured board, roll out the pastry to 3 mm /⅛ in thick. Cut a top for the pie slightly larger in size than the top of the dish. With the remaining pastry, cut strips 15 mm /½ in wide to line the rim of the dish.
4 Moisten the rim of the dish with water and press on the pastry strips all the way round. Brush this pastry rim with beaten egg and carefully lay the pastry on top of the pie, pressing the edges lightly together. Carefully brush off all the surface flour.
5 With the back of a sharp knife, knock up the edge of the pastry and then flute it all the way round. Cut a slit in the centre to allow the steam to escape. Score the pastry lightly in a diamond pattern with a knife. Leave it to relax for at least 30 minutes in the refrigerator.
6 Meanwhile, heat the oven to 220C /425F /gas 7.
7 Brush the pastry with egg to glaze. Bake the pie in the oven for 25–30 minutes or until the pastry is crisply puffed and golden.
8 Sprinkle the top of the pie with caster sugar and then serve it hot or lukewarm with thick cream.

● Freeze gooseberries when they are in season and cheap. Open freeze them without sugar and they will keep for 6–8 months.

Queen of puddings

 1½ hours

Serves 4

75 g /3 oz butter, softened
175 g /6 oz caster sugar
finely grated zest of 2 lemons
100 g /4 oz fresh white breadcrumbs
575 ml /1 pt milk
3 eggs, separated
250 g /8 oz strawberry jam

1 Heat the oven to 180C /350F /gas 4. Butter a medium-sized, heatproof pudding dish, about 25×18 cm /10×7 in, with 15 g / ½ oz of the softened butter.
2 Combine the remaining butter, 50 g /2 oz sugar and the grated lemon zest in a medium-sized mixing bowl. Beat well with a wooden spoon until the mixture is smooth and creamy, then stir in the fresh breadcrumbs.
3 In a small saucepan, scald the milk (bring to just under boiling point) over a moderate heat. Pour the milk over the butter and breadcrumb mixture in the bowl, stirring constantly with the wooden spoon. Set it aside and leave it to cool for 10 minutes.
4 With the spoon, beat the egg yolks into the mixture, one at a time. Pour the mixture into the prepared dish and bake it for 35–40 minutes or until the pudding is firm to the touch. Remove the dish from the oven and set it aside for 10 minutes to allow it to cool slightly.
5 With a spatula, spread the strawberry jam over the top of the cooled pudding. Reduce the oven temperature to 140C /275F /gas 1.
6 In a medium-sized mixing bowl, beat the egg whites with a clean wire whisk or a rotary beater until they form stiff peaks. Add 30 ml /1 tbls of the caster sugar and continue beating until the mixture is stiff and glossy.
7 With a large metal spoon, fold in the remaining caster sugar. Then, using a spatula, spread the meringue mixture over the pudding, fluffing up the surface into peaks with the spoon.
8 Return the dish to the oven and bake for 20–25 minutes or until the meringue has set and is golden brown on top.
9 Remove the pudding from the oven and serve immediately.

● Queen of puddings is a traditional English pudding that is both delicious and filling. If you use your own home-made strawberry jam, so much the better.

Queen of puddings

The Clever Cook

HOW TO CHEAT IN THE KITCHEN

Most cooks use convenience foods for everyday meals but may feel guilty when they include them in recipes for guests. Wisely used, they can provide shortcuts — so learn how to be a master of disguise in the kitchen!

Many people don't have the time to spend hours in the kitchen and therefore want reasonably speedy results when cooking. Others simply don't like having to prepare very complicated dishes — and cheerfully admit it! For both, there are two easy ways out.

Firstly, there is the no-cook or very-little-cooking approach — one everyone needs at some time or another. Get to know your local delicatessen and what their 'good buys' are. Keep an eye on what food is in season. At the height of the season fresh food is cheap, tasty and often needs little more than plain cooking and seasoning to be eaten at its best.

Secondly, there are convenience foods. A good many canned foods — for example, tuna — can be served without the tiniest feeling of guilt. Try tuna with oranges, grapes and mayonnaise for an unusual salad. It is a good example of the fact that with a little imagination and inventiveness convenience foods can be very useful indeed. Keep notes of your successful brand buys!

Starters
Here are some simple ideas to use for first courses:

Canned and packet soups: the different brands vary so greatly — even from flavour to flavour — that it is wise to experiment first, without guests, but all can be lifted by the discreet addition of some wine, sherry or brandy. A little cream, soured cream or butter stirred in just before serving is a good idea too, and finely chopped fresh herbs will add a home-made touch. Garnish clear soups with tiny croûtons; sprinkle paprika on pale soups and toasted sesame seeds on dark soups, and serve with crunchy French or garlic bread. A good tip is to blend packet soups briefly in a blender after heating them in order to elminate any tell-tale undissolved lumps.

Canned and bought dips and pâtés: mix in a little alcohol and cream cheese (for canned pâtés) and put into ramekins. Pour a little clarified butter over the top (see page 56) and put in the refrigerator to set — who is to say you didn't make it yourself? Add a little extra olive oil and lemon juice to canned hummus and taramasalata and sprinkle with freshly chopped parsley.

Main courses
Try some of these suggestions:

Sauces and dressings: a good sauce works wonders. Canned tomato sauces can be made to appear home-made by adding some sautéed chopped onion, mushrooms, olives, and finely chopped fresh basil. A spoonful of mushroom ketchup or one-quarter of a chicken stock cube helps to accentuate the flavours of any quick gravy.

Packet white sauces can be improved by adding a beaten egg yolk and a little cream. Heighten the flavour of cheese or mustard sauces by adding some extra cheese or stirring in some good French mustard. A generous sprinkling of freshly grated nutmeg helps many sauces.

Bought mayonnaise should also have an egg yolk added — to enrich the colour — plus a little olive oil and lemon juice to enhance the taste. Green herbs, capers or anchovies can be added to make various dressings.

Aspic and stuffings: aspic powder saves hours of work, but add a little sherry as part of the recommended quantity of liquid. Canned consommé is less satisfactory, as it tends to be too brown in colour. Dissolving gelatine in stock gives better results.

Packets of stuffing almost always betray their origins, so don't use them in large quantities. Add chopped fresh sage and parsley to them, with a little grated lemon zest and juice and freshly ground black pepper. If you have the time, chopped fresh onion or some cooked chestnuts will also improve them; chopped oranges or watercress are good too. Choose something which will accentuate the flavours of the dish and try to carry the theme over to the gravy or the accompanying vegetable or salad.

Canned meats, on the whole, usually taste like canned meat but there are a few exceptionally good brands. Even so, they can still be improved by adding fresh mushrooms, onions, tomatoes, herbs or spices and perhaps a little wine.

Canned curries can be lifted with some diced apple, onion and a little chutney stirred in, together with slices of fresh root ginger (cover with sherry and keep in the refrigerator — it will last for weeks). Coconut milk is a good addition too.

Potato: instant mashed potato is useful to thicken soups or as a binder for mixtures

such as fish croquettes or rissoles. Served as a vegetable, its origins may be difficult to conceal. If you have to use it, disguise it heavily with added cream or cream cheese and butter; this improves the appearance and texture as well as the taste. For a crunchy topping, sprinkle it with grated cheese and grill. Frozen chips can be quite successful because they end up being twice fried, in the same way as home-made French fries.

Other vegetables: frozen vegetables must be one of the most convenient forms of food ever invented, all ready prepared and tasting at their very best when cooked from frozen. Among canned vegetables broad beans, flageolets and petits pois are good as they are if reheated with butter and seasonings, and spinach can be successful too. Many other canned vegetables may be less attractive than their fresh cousins, although ratatouille reheated and served with soured cream makes an excellent side dish. There are some splendid brands of cooked red cabbage; add more chopped apple and a dash of vinegar with brown sugar when reheating this.

Where canned vegetables do come into their own is as a thickener. Purée them, then add to sauces or stews instead of a flour and butter mixture. Choose flavours with care — celery hearts are very good with fish, while mushrooms — particularly if mixed with some onions and blanched garlic — add flavour to beef and pork stews (especially canned ones).

Pastry: bought puff pastry is extremely convenient and invariably successful if you follow the instructions. Its one drawback is that it has no butter in it. To make it really light, roll it out once, dot 25 g /1 oz butter over two-thirds of the area and then fold and roll again. Leave folded in the refrigerator to rest for 10 minutes before rolling and shaping it. You can also use this procedure on shortcrust pastry which will make it extra rich and buttery. Bought pastry cases are also useful in emergencies.

Bread mixes have one great advantage over traditional dough — they need no first rise, so preparation time is much reduced. A shaped pizza base can rise while you prepare the topping. If you include an egg as part of the liquid when making the dough, the pizza

Spinach roulade and Carrot and apricot soup

can be kept warm in a low oven or be reheated without it becoming too leathery.

Desserts
Try using some of the following:
Frozen fruit, ready-prepared and waiting to go straight into pies or tarts, is another modern gift. But be selective: raspberries are very successful frozen, while strawberries are a disaster, fit only for puréeing.
Canned fruit also varies widely, pineapple being nearest in texture and taste to its fresh counterpart.

Don't serve canned fruit in their syrup, when their origin becomes obvious, but disguise them. Purée fruit to make a fruit sauce — for example, apricot sauce for cinnamon-flavoured banana fritters, or plum sauce for apple-filled crêpes. Or mix a purée with cream or yoghurt for a delicious fool. A beautifully rich ice cream can be made by blending peaches with some chopped hazelnuts and whipped cream and then freezing the mixture for 4–5 hours. Fruit juices (canned or frozen) make excellent sorbets.
Pie fillings: look for good brands among pie fillings (and consider whether frozen fruit would not be cheaper). Cherry pie filling is excellent inside pastry or crêpes, especially if extra frozen cherries are added.
Ice cream is universally popular and if you are able to buy dairy ice cream then you will have one less problem to worry about. However most ice cream sold in Britain is made of whipped vegetable fat and will never really be the same as home-made ice cream.
Biscuits: crush digestive biscuits to make a very quick flan base. Biscuits make marvellous desserts when soaked with alcohol (see Ginger cream log); or put broken biscuits into glasses and top with puréed fruit.

Carrot and apricot soup

 15–20 minutes

Serves 4
50 g /2 oz butter
1 small onion, grated
2 × 275 g /10 oz canned whole carrots, drained
212 g /7½ oz canned apricot halves and their syrup
600 ml /1 pt chicken or vegetable stock, home-made or from 1½ cubes
45 ml /3 tbls dry sherry
15 ml /1 tbls snipped fresh chives
salt and freshly ground black pepper
soured cream, to garnish (optional)

1 Melt the butter in a medium-sized saucepan and fry the onion over a low heat for 10 minutes, stirring frequently, until the onion is very soft and golden.
2 Meanwhile, put the drained carrots, the apricots and their syrup and the chicken or vegetable stock into the blender and blend until smooth.
3 Add the purée to the onions. Add the sherry, chives and salt and pepper. Heat the soup, stirring, but do not let it boil. Serve hot, garnished with soured cream, if liked.

Ham and nut rice

This versatile dish will make a main course for four or five and can be stretched, at a pinch, to feed eight. It is also easy to substitute most of the ingredients with other items (see below). Serve it with a green salad, if you have it, or with frozen green vegetables cooked and tossed in butter.

 30 minutes

Serves 4–5
salt
225 g /8 oz long-grain rice
15 ml /1 tbls olive oil
2 medium-sized onions, sliced
450 g /1 lb canned ham, cut into cubes and the can juices reserved
2.5 ml /½ tsp ground cinnamon
30 ml /2 tbls sherry or sweet vermouth
350 g /12 oz canned pineapple cubes or rings, drained (and cubed if necessary)
freshly ground black pepper
15 g /½ oz butter
a pinch of cayenne pepper
40 g /1½ oz almonds, blanched and flaked
finely chopped fresh parsley or a pinch of dried mixed herbs

1 Bring a pan of salted water to the boil and add the rice. Cover and simmer for 15 minutes.
2 Heat the olive oil in a frying-pan and soften half the onion slices. Add the ham cubes and toss until heated through. Sprinkle with the cinnamon and sherry or the vermouth. Add the pineapple cubes and the reserved juices from the ham. Season with salt and pepper and toss to warm the fruit.
3 In a small saucepan, heat the butter and fry the remaining onion slices over a medium heat until they colour.
4 Drain the rice, rinse and fluff it. Layer half into a large warmed serving dish, seasoning with salt and pepper and the smallest pinch of cayenne. Cover with half the ham and pineapple. Finish with a second layer of rice, seasoning as before. Top with the remaining ham and pineapple.
5 Sprinkle with the browned onion slices. Quickly toss the almonds in the remaining butter in the small pan. Top the dish with almonds and chopped parsley or a fine sprinkling of mixed herbs and serve.

● If you do not have a canned ham, substitute 225 g /8 oz bacon cut into stamp-sized squares. After adding the bacon to the onions, drain off the fat before proceeding. Hard boil 2 eggs and use these, chopped, to garnish.
● Substitute canned mandarin oranges for the canned pineapple.
● The canned pineapple can also be replaced by sultanas; use 175 g /6 oz and simmer them with the rice so that they plump up. Garnish the dish with the peeled segments of an orange for extra colour.
● Use whole peanuts instead of the flaked almonds, reducing or omitting the salt.
● As a rough and ready guide, for each additional person add 50 g /2 oz rice.

Spinach roulade

Serve two thin slices per person of this spinach-filled pastry for a starter or vegetable course, or three slices per person with a salad for a light lunch.

40 minutes, plus 1 hour 5 minutes baking

Serves 6–8
700 g /1½ lb frozen leaf spinach, defrosted
50 g /2 oz butter
1 large onion, finely chopped
1–2 garlic cloves, crushed
30 ml /2 tbls wine vinegar
5 ml /1 tsp sage
a pinch of nutmeg
salt
freshly ground black pepper
For the dough
butter, for greasing
200 ml /7 fl oz milk
550 ml /1 pt packet instant mashed potato
2 medium-sized eggs
1 medium-sized egg yolk
15 ml /1 tbls finely chopped fresh parsley
7.5 ml /1½ tsp salt
a good pinch of nutmeg
225 g /8 oz flour, plus extra for sprinkling
lightly beaten egg white, for brushing
To serve
watercress sprig (optional)
melted butter
freshly grated Parmesan cheese (optional)

1 To make the filling, put the spinach in a sieve and press out all the moisture. Melt the butter in a saucepan and cook the onion and garlic over a medium heat until it is soft and transparent.
2 Add the leaf spinach, wine vinegar, sage and nutmeg to the saucepan. Cook, stirring, for about 3 minutes, until the spinach is soft but the mixture is still moist. Season it to taste with salt and freshly ground black pepper.
3 To make the dough, heat the oven to 180C /350F /gas 4. Grease a large roasting pan. Put the milk in a saucepan with 225 ml /8 fl oz water and bring to the boil. Remove from the heat, add the potato powder or granules and beat with a wooden spoon until smooth. Allow to cool slightly.
4 Beat the eggs with the egg yolk, add to the potato and beat together vigorously. Mix in the parsley, salt and nutmeg. Gradually blend in the flour, stirring at first with the wooden spoon, then, when the mixture becomes stiffer, use one hand to mix in the flour. Knead lightly until smooth.
5 Lay a large sheet of greaseproof paper on the work surface and sprinkle it generously with flour. Roll the dough out on the paper to a 28 × 33 cm /11 × 13 in rectangle. Dust the surface of the dough with flour, if necessary, to prevent sticking.
6 Spread the spinach filling over the dough, leaving a 5 cm /2 in border on one of the long sides and a 25 mm /1 in border on the other 3 sides. Brush the borders with lightly beaten egg white. Roll the dough over

Cherries flambéed with kirsch

the filling, peeling back the paper and brushing excess flour from the dough. Roll the roulade off the paper and then into the roasting pan with the last roll. Pinch the seams and ends together. Brush any flour from the surface.
7 Bake for 65 minutes, until the roulade is cooked and golden. Slice into 15–20 mm /½–¾ in slices with a sharp knife and arrange on individual serving plates and garnish with watercress, if desired. For an extra rich flavour, serve with a little melted butter spooned over each individual portion. You could also provide a bowl of freshly grated Parmesan cheese, for sprinkling generously on top of the roulade.

Almond chicken puffs

These 'pillows' of puff pastry are filled with chicken breasts poached in white wine and served with a delicious, delicate-tasting almond and orange sauce. They make an impressive first course. Serve with a dry white wine, well chilled.

 1½ hours

Cherries flambéed with kirsch

 15–20 minutes

Serves 4
400 g /14 oz canned black cherries, stoned
a large pinch of ground cinnamon
30 ml /2 tbls caster sugar
150 g /5 oz redcurrant jelly
lemon juice (optional)
30–45 ml /2–3 tbls kirsch
600 ml /1 pt vanilla ice cream

1 Drain the canned black cherries through a sieve, reserving 150 ml /5 fl oz of the fruit syrup, and set aside.
2 In a small, heavy-based saucepan, combine the reserved fruit syrup with the ground cinnamon, sugar and redcurrant jelly. Set the pan over a low heat and bring the mixture gently to the boil. Reduce the heat and simmer the syrup gently, stirring occasionally, for 5 minutes.
3 Add the cherries and simmer gently for a further 2 minutes. Meanwhile, warm a deep, heatproof porcelain or copper-plated bowl.
4 When the cherries are hot, but not disintegrating, transfer them to the heated bowl using a slotted spoon. Taste the syrup and sharpen the flavour with a little lemon juice if necessary. Pour the syrup over the cherries.
5 Pour the kirsch into a metal ladle and then warm it over a low heat. Taking very great care, set light to the kirsch and, when flaming, pour it over the cherries. Serve before the flames die down, accompanied by vanilla ice cream.

Ginger cream log

25 minutes,
then 8 hours chilling

Serves 6
300 ml /10 fl oz whipping cream
60–75 ml /4–5 tbls medium dry sherry
175 g /6 oz ginger biscuits
2 pieces stem ginger, drained and sliced

1 Select a long, oval-shaped serving dish. Whip the cream until thick. Pour the sherry into a wide, shallow bowl.
2 As you need them, dip the biscuits in the sherry for 5 seconds on each side, then put a spoonful of whipped cream on each biscuit, using about a third of the cream in all, and sandwich them together to form a log on the serving dish.
3 Reserve a little cream for the decoration. Mask the log with the remainder of the cream, swirling it in an attractive pattern.
4 Put the reserved cream in a piping bag fitted with a large star nozzle and pipe a line of scrolls along the top of the log. Place a slice of ginger diagonally into the cream on either side of each cream scroll.
5 Refrigerate for at least 8 hours; but remember that after 24 hours the cream will discolour. To serve, slice diagonally.

Serves 4
150 ml /5 fl oz dry white wine
10 white peppercorns
1 small onion, coarsely chopped
4 sprigs of parsley
1 garlic clove
4 chicken breasts, boned and with the skin removed
4 large oranges
175 g /6 oz butter
50 g /2 oz fresh breadcrumbs
100 g /4 oz ground almonds
225 g /8 oz frozen puff pastry, defrosted
flour, for dusting
1 egg yolk, beaten
butter, for greasing
50 g /2 oz blanched whole almonds
salt
100 g /4 oz thick cream

1 Put the wine, white peppercorns, onion, parsley and whole garlic clove into a large saucepan and add 1.1 L /2 pt cold water. Bring to the boil. Add the chicken breasts and simmer gently for 15–20 minutes until the breasts are almost cooked.
2 Remove the chicken and cool.
3 Add the grated zest of one orange to the stock in the pan. Boil the stock hard until it is reduced to 275 ml /10 fl oz, then strain.

4 Melt 125 g /4 oz butter in a large frying-pan and add the breadcrumbs, stirring so that all the crumbs are coated with butter and evenly browned. Put into a blender with the ground almonds and stock and blend.
5 Squeeze the juice from 3 oranges and add it to the sauce, which should be quite thick. Heat the oven to 220C /425F /gas 7.
6 Divide the pastry into 4 and, using a lightly-floured rolling pin and board, roll out each portion into a 15 cm /6 in square. Place a chicken breast in the centre of each portion and spoon 10 ml /2 tsp of the sauce over each breast. Fold over the pastry to form an envelope and seal. Brush the edges with beaten egg yolk and place the envelopes on a greased baking sheet. Bake for 20–25 minutes.
7 Melt the remaining butter in the frying-pan and sauté the blanched almonds until evenly browned. Drain them on absorbent paper, sprinkle with salt and reserve.
8 Peel the remaining orange, removing all the pith, and cut into 8 thin slices. If there is any orange juice on the plate, add it to the sauce and stir to blend thoroughly.
9 Put the chicken puffs on a serving plate and keep warm while finishing the sauce.
10 Add the cream to the remaining sauce, stir well and pour over the chicken. Put 2 orange slices on each envelope, sprinkle with the almonds and serve at once.

AWAY-FOR-THE-DAY COOKING

How wonderful to return after a day's work and find a hot meal waiting for you! All you have to do is put a slow-cooking meal in the oven when you leave in the morning — and your part of the work is done.

What is to be gained by cooking for a minimum of eight hours when instant or freezer food can be turned into a meal in minutes? The answer is economy and a better flavoured and more nourishing meal at the end. Slow cooking lets you leave the kitchen after very little preparation, while the cooking takes care of itself. In an oven heated to the lowest possible temperature the food will cook safely for eight hours or more in a reliable oven. (Have your oven checked if it is old and/or temperamental.) Even if you are delayed in returning home, the food will maintain a constant temperature and will not dry out or burn. There can hardly be a more carefree method of cooking!

Most quickly cooked meat dishes require expensive cuts of meat and, usually, a certain amount of skill and judgement from the cook. Not so with slow cooking, which comes into its own when the family wants a good old-fashioned casserole or hearty stew. Nothing could be simpler than stewing meat and vegetables in a pot. Slow cooking is exactly what is needed to transform the more economical cuts of meat, like neck of lamb, shin of beef and pork belly, or offal, like liver and tongue, into gorgeous, appetizing dishes. Tough sinews are broken down during long, slow cooking and the meat juices make a thick, tasty gravy. Meat and vegetables to be cooked this way do not even need to be fried before being put in the casserole, so preparation time is kept to the bare minimum.

No special equipment

You do not need special equipment for slow cooking. Although you can buy electric slow cookers or 'crock pots' which are economical on fuel, a conventional home oven will do the same job without any extra capital outlay.

Fill up the oven with several dishes to make the best use of fuel, then freeze the extra dishes to save even more time at a later date. Use improvized containers if you do not own more than one casserole. Cake tins and saucepans can be used; at this low temperature plastic or composition handles and knobs will come to no harm.

Experiment with your oven the first time you try slow cooking: the lowest possible setting varies from one manufacturer to another. Set the oven at the nearest mark to 85C /180F /gas Low, and cook for about eight hours. Adjust the temperature according to the result. Shelf positions will also make a difference and the location of the elements or burners. Do remember that the floor of the oven can also be used.

What to cook

Most casseroles and stews can be slow cooked, following your favourite recipes, as long as there is sufficient liquid to cover the meat and vegetables. As well as the cheaper cuts of meat, root vegetables can be slow cooked, either as part of a casserole or on their own in liquid. Pulses can be slow cooked efficiently, although they still need preliminary soaking and you should bring them to the boil in their cooking liquid before putting them into a slow oven. Potatoes and rice can also be cooked this way, as can dried fruit, which needs no preliminary soaking.

Slow roasting meat

Both meat and poultry can be slow roasted and a meat thermometer is an aid to success. If you are not pot-roasting in liquid, try wrapping the meat in cooking foil, and push the thermometer in at the thickest part, away from the bone. Stand the wrapped meat package on a rack in the pan. Seal the meat by cooking in a hot oven, 200C /400F /gas 6, for 15 minutes to kill any surface bacteria before slow roasting at the lower temperature of 85C /180F /gas low. Before serving the meat, it can be browned by removing the wrapping and raising the temperature to very hot, 240C /475F /gas 9, for 15 minutes.

Slow-cooked cassoulet

Making a classic French cassoulet can be a lengthy process, but when the meat and beans are slow cooked separately in the oven at the same time, the preparations are speeded up. Cooking the meat separately also prevents the fat running into the bean juices, thus making the dish less rich. It reheats well.

overnight soaking, then 9–10 hours

Serves 8–10
1 small oven-ready duck
30 ml /2 tbls clear honey
1 large breast of lamb, boned, rolled and tied
500 g /1 lb belly pork, in one piece
salt and freshly ground black pepper
500 g /1 lb white haricot beans, soaked overnight in cold water
1 large onion, cut into eight and each section stuck with a whole clove
2 celery sticks, chopped
2–4 garlic cloves, crushed
60 ml /4 tbls tomato purée
30 ml /2 tbls black treacle
10 ml /2 tsp prepared French mustard
bouquet garni
250 g /8 oz piece of garlic sausage, chopped into bite-sized pieces
freshly chopped parsley, to garnish

1 Heat the oven to 85C /180F /gas Low. Put the duck on a large rack in a roasting tin and brush the skin with the honey. Put the lamb and pork on the rack next to the duck and sprinkle both poultry and meat liberally with salt and pepper.
2 Drain the beans and place them in a deep flameproof casserole. Add the onion, celery and garlic. Mix together the tomato purée, treacle and mustard with a little of 1.2 L /2 pt boiling water, then pour into the casserole with the remaining water. Next, add the bouquet garni.
3 Bring to the boil on top of the stove, then cover with a lid and transfer to the bottom of the oven. Place the duck and meat in the oven above the beans.
4 Cook for at least 8 hours until the beans and meat are tender.
5 Remove the duck and meats from the oven, and pour off the fat from the bottom of the roasting tin. Divide the duck into serving portions or carve the flesh from the bones. Cut the lamb and pork into bite-sized pieces, discarding any large pieces of fat and rind.
6 Remove the bouquet garni from the beans and discard. Stir the meat into the beans, together with the garlic sausage. Transfer to the top of the stove and cook for a further 30 minutes, adding a little water if the beans become dry.

Slow-cooked cassoulet

7 Adjust the seasoning, then sprinkle with the parsley and serve.

● Half a shoulder of lamb, shank or lean end, can be substituted for the duck.

Beef in Guinness

Any root vegetable in season may be added to this casserole along with the carrots — and the butter beans may be omitted.

8–9 hours

Serves 4–6
45 ml /3 tbls flour
2.5 ml /½ tsp mustard powder
salt and freshly ground black pepper
1.25 kg /2½ lb stewing beef, cubed
1 small onion, finely chopped
2 celery sticks, finely chopped
2 medium-sized carrots, finely chopped
2 garlic cloves, crushed
75 g /3 oz butter beans, soaked
15–30 ml /1–2 tbls dark soft brown sugar
300 ml /11 fl oz Guinness
1 bouquet garni

1 Heat the oven to 85C /180F /gas Low.
2 Put the flour, mustard and seasoning in a plastic bag and shake the meat cubes in it to coat them all over. Put the meat in a large casserole and add the chopped onion, celery, carrots, garlic, butter beans and soft brown sugar to taste. Add the Guinness and 150 ml /5 fl oz water. Stir well to mix. Push the bouquet garni into the centre of the ingredients.
2 Cover with a lid and cook in the oven for about 8 hours.
3 Before serving, remove the bouquet garni, stir well and adjust the seasoning.

● For slow-cooked mashed potatoes to serve with Beef in Guinness, place finely-sliced old potatoes in a shallow casserole dish with plenty of salt and pepper. Cover with milk and top with a knob of butter. Cover and slow cook for 8 hours with the casserole, then mash well before serving.

Pâté de campagne

Mincing raw meat and liver when making home-made pâté can be an arduous task. Slow cooking the ingredients first, though, means that they can be quickly worked to a smooth texture — either in a blender or a vegetable mill. This 'country' pâté can be as fine or as coarse as you like, depending on the length of time the meat is blended or how many times it is put through the mill.

8–9 hours,
plus 2 chilling periods

Makes about 12 slices
500 g /1 lb boned pork spare rib, cubed
500 g /1 lb fat belly pork, cubed with the rind reserved
250 g /9 oz pig's liver, chopped
500 g /1 lb shin of beef, cubed
300 ml /11 fl oz red wine
1 medium-sized onion, finely chopped
2 garlic cloves, crushed
5 ml /1 tsp dried thyme
2 bay leaves
salt and freshly ground black pepper

1 Start making this pâté a day or more before you plan to serve it. Heat the oven to 85C /180F /gas Low. Put all the ingredients in a casserole, placing the reserved pork rind on the top. Cook, uncovered, in the oven for at least 8 hours, until the meats are tender, and the juices are pale yellow rather than pink in colour.
2 Remove from the oven, leave to cool, then chill in the refrigerator until the fat solidifies on top of the meat.
3 Remove and discard the fat and pork rind, then strain the liquid off the meat, reserving a little.
4 Work the meat in an electric blender or vegetable mill with the reserved liquid, then press into a foil-lined 2 L /3 pt loaf tin or mould. Press down well, cover and place weights on top.
5 Chill in the refrigerator until firm, then slice and serve.

Pork vindaloo

The traditional method of making this Indian curry is to marinate the meat in vinegar overnight. Slow cooking allows you to cook the pork in vinegar without marinating first.

8–9 hours

Serves 4–6
1.25 kg /2½ lb boned pork spare rib, cubed
100 ml /3½ fl oz wine vinegar
2 garlic cloves, crushed
2.5 cm /1 in piece of fresh root ginger, crushed
15 ml /1 tbls mustard seeds, crushed
10 ml /2 tsp ground coriander
10 ml /2 tsp ground cumin
150 ml /5 fl oz chicken stock, home-made or from a cube

1 Heat the oven to 85C /180F /gas Low. Place the pork cubes in a large casserole dish. Mix together the remaining ingredients and pour them over the pork.
2 Cover and cook in the oven for about 8 hours. Stir well before serving.

● If mustard seeds are difficult to obtain, use French mustard which has whole seeds in it.
● Serve slow-cooked rice with Pork vindaloo: heat a little oil in a flameproof casserole dish and add 100 g /4 oz long-grain rice and fry until golden. Pour in 450 ml /16 fl oz boiling chicken stock or water and stir once. Cover tightly and slow cook it in the oven with the pork dish for about 8 hours.
● Substitute a boned-out shoulder of lamb, in cubes, for the pork spare rib.

DOUBLING UP THE DINNER

Everyone has been faced with extra unexpected supper guests at some time. Find out how a few items from your store cupboard, plus a little ingenuity, can turn a meal for two into an impressive dinner for four.

Cubed and minced meat dishes are easy to extend in order to feed extra mouths. Just add more vegetables, chopped fried bacon, rice or pasta. Much more difficult to deal with — though not impossible — are meals which have been planned so that each person has one portion of meat or fish.

For starters

If you can make a fairly substantial starter, filling up everyone with the first course, then small quantities of meat or fish in the main course will not be so noticeable. Cans of vegetables such as carrots, peas, butter or kidney beans and tomatoes are a marvellous standby. A quick turn in a blender, a little stock added (or half a stock cube and some water), a few herbs, a dash of cream (or top of the milk) and you have a delicious soup. Frozen chopped spinach or cauliflower florets are also perfect for turning into soups. Make some garlic bread and serve with the soup. Add 1–2 finely chopped garlic cloves and 15–30 ml /1–2 tbls freshly chopped parsley to 100 g /4 oz softened butter and pound into a smooth paste. Keeping the base intact, cut a French loaf into slices and spread the butter mixture on each slice. Wrap the loaf in tin foil and bake for 20 minutes at 220C /25F /gas 7.

Pasta makes quick, filling starters; serve it simply (and authentically) tossed in olive oil and crushed garlic, or with bacon and egg *alla carbonara*. Or purée the contents of a can of tomatoes, mix with a little cream and a good pinch of dried basil to make a pretty pink sauce. Buy green tagliatelle and keep it in reserve with a can of peeled shrimps. Sauté the shrimps in butter, then add cream for a delicious sauce to serve with the pasta.

Canned pimentoes, drained, chopped and mixed with anchovy fillets, dressed with olive oil and lots of freshly ground black pepper, and served with bread and butter, also make an unusual starter.

Last but not least, there are eggs. A simple omelette with a few herbs added, or eggs baked in the oven, topped with herbs and cream, are both delicious. Or hard boil the eggs and top them with mayonnaise and some mock caviar (lumpfish roe). If you have a can of tuna fish, make an egg and tuna salad, top it with a little 'caviar' and serve it on a bed of finely sliced onions.

Main course ideas

This is the problem area, but a little imagination can make small quantities of food go further. Fish presents the least problems. Turn white or smoked fish fillets into a kedgeree or pie. Both rice and onions should be a mainstay of your kitchen; if you have the odd can of tuna, salmon, shrimps, crab or even sardines (provided you rinse them under hot water to remove their oil), they can all be added to pad out the dish. A whole fish, like trout, can be split in half and topped with a rich stuffing and sauce (see Shrimp and almond trout).

Pork chops are not the problem you may imagine. Cut out the bone and chop the meat into bite-sized cubes and make kebabs, pilaus or a curry. Or cook the pork with garlic and coriander seeds in milk (see recipe), then serve with sauté potatoes.

Chicken breasts need a little more ingenuity. Chop the meat, mix it with some sautéed onion and mushrooms (open a can) and with a little white sauce. If you have time to defrost some puff pastry, divide the filling among squares of pastry, bake and serve with more white sauce. Or use the filling to stuff onions (see recipe), large baking tomatoes, crêpes or omelettes.

If you have bought thick rump or fillet steaks, slice them in half through the middle to make four thinner ones. Make a peppercorn sauce and serve with lots of mashed potatoes. Or roll your thin steaks around some liver pâté and make a wine-enriched brown sauce with a few chopped olives or capers. Brown the steaks under a very hot grill with breadcrumbs or a little grated cheese sprinkled on top.

For the dessert

Tins of fruit such as gooseberries, raspberries, blackberries, guavas, apricots, plums or pineapples can all be used to produce delicious sweets (see Cherries flambéed with kirsch, page 29). Long-life or UHT cream is invaluable as a topping. Whisk it with a little icing sugar and some liqueur, brandy or whisky until soft peaks form and pile it on the fruit. A mixture of drained canned fruit and fresh fruit makes a quick pudding and appears more creative than just opening a can.

Baked apples, oranges or plums topped with cream also make delicious hot puddings. Canned half peaches, drained and heated in a caramel sauce, taste so much better than plain cold ones. Fruit crumbles are both quick to make and always well-received.

Onions stuffed with chicken

Onions stuffed with chicken

 30–45 minutes

Serves 4
4 medium-sized onions
salt
2 chicken breasts, boned and skinned
50 g /2 oz butter, plus extra for greasing
100 g /3½ oz canned button mushrooms,
*   drained*
30 ml /2 tbls finely chopped fresh parsley
*   or 15 ml /1 tbls dried parsley*
freshly ground black pepper
30 ml /2 tbls dried breadcrumbs
225 g /8 oz tagliatelle verdi
15 ml /1 tbls tomato purée
75 ml /3 fl oz dry white wine

1 Peel the onions but keep them whole. Fill a large pan with salted water, bring to the boil, drop in the onions and parboil for 5 minutes. Remove the onions with a slotted spoon onto a plate.
2 Carefully take out the middle of the onions, leaving about three outer layers of skin on each one. Reserve these outer layers

and then finely chop the rest of the onions.
3 Chop the chicken breasts into matchstick-size strips and set aside.
4 Melt 40 g /1½ oz butter in a heavy-based frying-pan over a moderate heat, add the chopped onion and sauté until it is soft and golden, about 4–5 minutes. Add the chopped chicken breast meat and sauté for a further 2 minutes. Add the mushrooms and parsley, season with salt and freshly ground black pepper and stir for 3 minutes.
5 Heat the oven to 190C /375F /gas 5. Using a teaspoon, carefully stuff each onion with a quarter of the chicken breast mixture. Grease a baking tray and place the stuffed onions on the tray. Sprinkle 7.5 ml /1½ tbls dried breadcrumbs over each onion, dot with the remaining butter and put in the oven for 20 minutes.
6 Meanwhile, bring a large pan of salted water to the boil and drop in the tagliatelle. Cook fairly briskly for 15–20 minutes until the tagliatelle is cooked but still *al dente*.
7 Mix the tomato purée with the white wine in a small bowl. Drain the tagliatelle, return to the pan off the heat and toss in the tomato purée and wine mixture. Season with salt and freshly ground black pepper. Put the tagliatelle onto a warmed serving platter.
8 Remove the stuffed onions from the oven, arrange on the tagliatelle and serve.

● If you find it easier, sauté the chicken breasts whole for 4 minutes, remove them from the pan, take out the bone and then chop the meat finely.

Coriander pork in milk

Pork simmered in milk, with onions, smoked bacon and petits pois will make a succulent, tasty and unusual dish.

 1–1¼ hours

Serves 4
2 pork loin chops
50 g /2 oz butter
2 large onions, finely chopped
4 slices smoked bacon, chopped (optional)
225 g /8 oz canned petits pois, drained
16 coriander seeds
1 garlic clove, finely chopped
salt and freshly ground black pepper
300 ml /10 fl oz milk
sautéed potatoes, to serve
finely chopped fresh parsley, to garnish

1 Cut the pork into bite-sized pieces, removing as much flesh from the bone as possible.
2 Melt the butter in a large saucepan over a moderate heat, add the onions, and sauté until soft and transparent, about 5 minutes. Add the chopped smoked bacon, if using, and the pork and stir for 2 minutes.
3 Add the peas, coriander seeds, garlic, salt and freshly ground black pepper. Stir everything together well, then cover with the milk. Turn the heat down slightly and simmer, uncovered for 30 minutes.

4 Stir everything once more. The milk should have formed a cobweb over the pan — stir this well in and simmer for a further 20 minutes or until the milk has reduced to a rich, thick sauce.
5 Pile the meat mixture into the middle of a warmed serving platter, surround with sautéed potatoes, sprinkle with parsley and serve at once.

Shrimp and almond trout

A can of shrimps, one of button mushrooms and a few flaked almonds can soon transform two trout into a delicious meal for four.

 30 minutes

Serves 4
2 × 350 g /12 oz trout, cleaned, defrosted if
*   frozen*
150 ml /5 fl oz dry white wine
2 bay leaves
6 white peppercorns
50 g /2 oz butter
100 g /3½ oz canned button mushrooms,
*   drained and finely chopped*
175 g /6 oz canned peeled shrimps, drained
juice of ½ lemon
150 ml /5 fl oz thick cream
salt and freshly ground black pepper
cooked leaf spinach, to serve
50 g /2 oz flaked almonds
mashed potato, to serve

1 With sharp kitchen scissors, slit each trout, open out flat and cut each one in half lengthways.
2 Place the fish in a pan large enough to hold them in one layer and just cover with water. Add the wine, bay leaves and peppercorns. Bring the liquid to the boil, then simmer gently for 10–15 minutes until the fish flakes easily with a fork.
3 Meanwhile, melt 40 g /1½ oz butter in a frying-pan, add the drained mushrooms and sauté for 3–4 minutes. Remove them from the pan with a slotted spoon and keep hot.
4 Add the peeled shrimps to the pan, together with the lemon juice, and sauté them for 5 minutes. Stir in the cream, season with salt and freshly ground black pepper and stir for a further 2 minutes without allowing the sauce to boil. Turn the heat to its lowest possible setting.
5 Carefully remove the fish from the pan, put on a warmed serving platter on top of a bed of spinach. Gently ease away the backbones and all smaller bones.
6 Cover each fish half with some of the mushrooms, then pour the sauce over them. Keep the fish hot.
7 Melt the remaining butter in the frying-pan and sauté the flaked almonds for 1–2 minutes. When they are golden brown, sprinkle over the fish and serve immediately with lots of mashed potato.

● For an unusual variation, substitute clams for the peeled shrimps and chopped hazelnuts for the almonds.

STOP-THE-CLOCK DINNERS

That perfect meal, carefully planned and cooked, can easily be ruined by the late arrival of one guest. Many dishes, however, can be partly cooked, then finished at the last minute, enabling you to produce a meal without worry.

If you have guests who are likely to arrive an hour late or family who announce they will be back for lunch and arrive at tea-time — starving, naturally — the obvious answer is to use your microwave oven (see pages 60–63), but if you have not got one, then a casserole in the oven may be the answer.

There are many delicious and unusual casseroles to choose from, such as Pork hot-pot (page 12) or Beef in Guinness (page 31) or, for a lovely warming winter supper, Slow-cooked cassoulet (page 30). However, if you want to produce something rather grander for a more formal dinner party, then some careful advance planning is required.

Make-ahead starters

The first problem area to deal with is the starter. Plan something that can be cooked in advance and served cold, or kept warm until serving time, or reheated.

Pâtés can be made well in advance and are always popular. There are many to choose from, such as Pâté de campagne (page 31). Both salads and antipasto platters keep well, covered, in the refrigerator. A mousse is an elegant start to a dinner party. Do remember to take the mousses out of the refrigerator once all your guests have arrived, to remove the chill.

Chicken timbales (page 20) make an impressive starter and can be kept warm in their moulds until you are ready to turn them out. Soups can be kept warm or reheated, depending on their ingredients (see pages 8–9), while flans or quiches can often be served at any temperature: try the recipe for Cheese and tomato tart (page 11).

Main courses

Apart from the obvious answer of casseroles, there are many other dishes which — with a little planning — can be adapted to waiting for a late arrival.

You don't need to worry about salmon being ruined if you keep it (either a whole fish or steaks) in the poaching liquid, which can then be quickly reduced to make a delicious sauce (see recipe).

Sometimes the sauce can be cooked first, as in Veal escalopes with chicken liver sauce (see recipe): make the chicken liver purée for the sauce in advance, then finish the sauce off at the last minute while you sauté the veal.

If you don't want to be tied to the kitchen stove at all once everyone has arrived, try Lamb steaks braised in wine (see recipe). This is an easy to prepare dish which becomes more delicious the longer it is left, the sauce becoming thicker and richer while the lamb stays juicy and succulent. Keep the oven low while you are waiting, then turn it up at the end for 10 minutes to make sure the meat is really hot.

There are, of course, also dishes which can be cooked completely in well under 30 minutes. Particularly delicious and unusual is Mackerel with gooseberry sauce (page 10), a light and pretty *nouvelle cuisine* dish. Trout meunière, where the trout is seasoned, lightly floured and then fried in butter, is a classic and one of the tastiest ways to serve fresh trout.

Potatoes and other root vegetables can be kept warm in a very low oven, covered with greaseproof paper to stop them drying out, while salads should be put in the refrigerator or covered with cling film. If using a mayonnaise or oil and vinegar dressing, dress the salads only just before serving, otherwise they will quickly become soggy in texture.

Sorbets, ice creams, moulded jellies, cold soufflés and mousses (see Prune and orange mousse, page 22) all make ideal desserts, as they can be cooked the day before or on the morning of the dinner party and left in the refrigerator until 30 minutes before you serve them.

A compote of black fruit adds a sophisticated touch to the meal, as does Ginger peach sundae (page 22). Serve Cherries flambéed with kirsch (page 29) or a meringue basket with fresh fruit and ice cream for a trouble-free finish to your meal.

Salmon steaks with lime and pine nuts

40 minutes

Serves 4

4 × 175 g /6 oz salmon steaks
1 small onion, finely chopped
2 bay leaves
6 white peppercorns
15 ml /1 tbls dry vermouth
5 ml /1 tsp dried savory
zest of 1 lime
lime slices, to garnish
For the sauce
25 g /1 oz butter
15 ml /1 tbls pine nuts
15 ml /1 tbls flour
juice of 1 lime
2 medium-sized egg yolks
150 ml /5 fl oz thick cream
salt and freshly ground black pepper

1 Put the salmon into a pan large enough to hold the steaks in a single layer. Add the

Salmon steaks with lime and pine nuts

onion, bay leaves, peppercorns, vermouth, savory and lime zest. Pour in enough cold water to cover.
2 Bring to the boil over a medium-low heat, then turn down the heat and simmer gently for 5–6 minutes. If they are not required immediately, leave the steaks in their poaching liquid. They can then be reheated by quickly bringing the liquid to the boil and boiling for 1 minute.
3 Remove the steaks carefully with a slotted spoon to a warmed serving platter, cover them with foil and keep them warm while you make the sauce.
4 Reduce the poaching liquid over a high heat until you have 175 ml /6 fl oz. Strain the liquid into a jug and put the jug into a bowl of iced water to cool it slightly.
5 In a heavy-based frying-pan, melt half the butter over a moderate heat. When it bubbles, turn down the heat and add the pine nuts. Sauté for about 2 minutes, until they are golden, shaking the pan from time to time. Remove with a slotted spoon, drain on absorbent paper and reserve.
6 In a small saucepan, melt the remaining butter over a medium heat, then add the flour, stirring constantly to make a roux. Gradually pour in the cooled stock, still stirring. Bring it to the boil and cook, stirring, for 2–3 minutes. Add the lime juice and mix well.
7 Whisk the egg yolks with the cream in a bowl and gradually pour this into the pan, whisking all the time. Season to taste with salt and pepper, add the pine nuts and simmer for 2 minutes, but do not allow the sauce to come to the boil.
8 Remove the foil from the salmon steaks, pour the sauce over them, then garnish with the lime slices and serve at once.

Lamb steaks braised in wine

 1 hour 40 minutes

Serves 4

4 lamb steaks from the leg, about 25 mm /
* 1 in thick*
4 garlic cloves
salt and freshly ground black pepper
5 ml /1 tsp ground allspice
50 g /2 oz butter
2 medium-sized onions, thinly sliced
2 medium-sized cooking apples, thinly sliced
2 sprigs of rosemary
300 ml /11 fl oz red wine

1 Heat the oven to 180C /350F /gas 4. Rub the lamb steaks on both sides with a garlic clove, season with salt and pepper and dust with the allspice.
2 Melt the butter in a flameproof casserole large enough to take the steaks in a single layer. Add the onions and cook over a low heat for 5 minutes, until they are soft but not coloured. Remove them from the pan.
3 Add the apple slices to the casserole and sauté for 1–2 minutes on each side. Remove them with a slotted spoon. Add the lamb steaks to the pan and sauté them over a high

heat for 2 minutes each side to seal them.
4 Return the onions and apples to the dish, covering the steaks. Add the whole garlic cloves and the rosemary. Pour in the wine, adding a little water if necessary to cover, and cook, covered with a tightly fitting lid, in the oven for 30 minutes.
5 Turn the oven down to 130C /250F /gas ½. Baste the steaks with the wine and cook for a further 30 minutes.
6 Remove the steaks from the casserole with a slotted spoon, discarding the rosemary and returning any pieces of apple or onion to the juices.
7 Let the juices cool slightly, spoon off any fat that rises to the top, then liquidize the juices in a blender and return to the casserole with the lamb steaks.
8 Return the casserole to the oven for another 10 minutes to reheat the meat, then either serve at once or turn the oven down very low to keep the casserole warm, then turn it up to 190C /375F /gas 5 for 10 minutes before serving.

Veal escalopes with chicken liver sauce

30 minutes

Serves 6

75 g /3 oz butter
225 g /8 oz chicken livers
30 ml /2 tbls dry Madeira
150 ml /5 fl oz dry rosé or white wine
150 ml /5 fl oz strong beef stock, home-made
* or from a cube, plus extra if needed*
6 veal escalopes
10 ml /2 tsp fresh dill, finely chopped
salt
freshly ground black pepper
150 ml /5 fl oz soured cream
2–3 dashes Worcestershire sauce
sprigs of dill, to garnish

1 Melt 50 g /2 oz butter in a large, heavy-based frying-pan over medium heat, add the chicken livers and sauté for 3–4 minutes, until they are firm on the outside but still pink inside. Remove from the pan with a slotted spoon and reserve.
2 Add the Madeira and wine to the pan, scraping up any crusty bits with a wooden spoon, then add the stock. Stir well, then remove from the heat.
3 Put the chicken livers into a blender with the liquid from the pan and purée, or sieve them, then add the liquid gradually to make a smooth purée.
4 Melt the remaining butter in the frying-pan and sauté the veal escalopes in 2 batches for 2–3 minutes on each side. Remove from the pan, place on a warmed serving platter, overlapping them, and keep warm.
5 Return the chicken liver purée to the pan, add the chopped dill and season with salt and pepper. Stir in the soured cream, add 2–3 dashes of Worcestershire sauce, and a little more stock if the sauce is too thick. Bring it just to boiling point, then pour it over the escalopes. Garnish with sprigs of dill and serve at once.

TWO-TIER MEALS

Save yourself time and trouble when you have a house full of guests — serve a 'split' dinner using the same basic ingredients as a starting point, but keeping flavours simple for the children and spiced up for the adults.

'Split meals' are the obvious answer to Saturday night entertaining when you have guests staying for the weekend with their children. There are many things which can be presented simply for the children and then transformed into a grand dinner party dish, perhaps with the addition of some alcohol, a few herbs or spices, or a sauce. Here are some ideas that aim to please all tastes without entailing hours in the kitchen.

First course
The starter should present no problems: children will usually be content with a main course and a dessert, so you have a free hand to choose the appetizer. It is wise though to plan something which can be cooked in advance or even the day before. Pâtés and terrines are ideal as they actually benefit from 2–3 days maturing before they are eaten, so you can do the cooking earlier in the week. Try Liver and hazelnut pâté (see page 64), or Mousse of smoked mackerel (see page 103). Citrus cocktail (see page 81) is light and refreshing and so is Japanese beef with fresh ginger (see page 96) which needs the minimum amount of preparation.

Main course
Children usually like simple ingredients cooked in a straightforward way, so fish, beef or chicken all provide ideal starting points for planning your main course.

Some children find fish dull but few will say no to fish cakes or fish pie with a creamy or cheesy mashed potato topping. You can then treat the adults to Cod, spinach and cheese bake (see page 47). Serve the children frozen or fresh peas as a vegetable accompaniment and the adults Glazed peas (see recipe) with their meal.

Beef probably gives you the most choice for children and adults alike. You can mince part of a joint to feed the children. However, if you are buying mince for everyone, try making a tasty bolognese sauce and serving it with spaghetti or pasta shapes, or Baked Surprise potatoes, with their rich, meaty filling and cheese topping. Both dishes will be popular with the young, and can be easily adapted for more mature palates with the addition of wine and garlic (see recipe).

Hamburgers will go down well with youngsters and, again, more sophisticated tastes can be catered for with Gourmet hamburgers (see page 18). Serve them with Boiled or sautéed new potatoes (see recipe). Boil enough potatoes for everyone, then present them plain-boiled to the children, and sautéed in butter to the adults. A simple lettuce and tomato salad is an ideal accompaniment for younger tastes; adults will appreciate tangy Orange and chicory salad (see page 109).

Children's meal: Tomato-painted chicken legs and Rhubarb oatmeal crumble

Other 'adult' beef ideas are thin slices rolled around prunes that have been soaked in brandy. Or try the Madeira sauce (see page 46) which is more usually served with ham but makes a lovely accompaniment to beef.

Chicken also gives a wide variety of choices and is universally appealing. Roast chicken legs are especially popular with children as they can eat them with their fingers. If you 'paint' them with tomato ketchup, as in Tomato-painted chicken legs (see recipe), it gives the skin a sweet crunchy taste — even more appealing. Or coat the legs in batter or egg and roll them in breadcrumbs, then deep-fry them for another popular dish. Have plenty of napkins at hand, serve with tomato sauce and relishes, and your early eaters will be quite satisfied.

If you buy 2 chickens, cut off the legs for the children's meal and use the breasts to make a meal for the adults. If you know your guests like garlic, then Chicken Kiev is the popular classic to try. Chicken breasts cooked with mushrooms in puff pastry (see recipe) make a melt-in-the-mouth dish, while Chicken kebabs with peanut sauce (see page 47) are delicious, with their spicy and unusual dressing. There are several other suggestions for using chicken in other chapters of this book.

Fish, beef or chicken can be minced or finely chopped and mixed with a sauce to make a delicious filling for crêpes. As the crêpes can be made ahead of time, their versatility becomes even more useful. Serve them filled with cooked minced beef and bechamel sauce for the children's main course. For the adults they make a super first course; seafood crêpes filled with lobster,

mussels or any other available fish, or avocado pancakes are good ideas.

Desserts

Ice cream must spring to mind as the first answer for a dessert. Popular with old and young, it can be kept at hand in the freezer and involves no cooking at all on the day of the meal. Peppermint and chocolate ice cream is usually a firm favourite for the children; for the adults, serve it with a little Crème de menthe or chocolate mint liqueur. Crumbles are another childhood love and can be varied according to what fruit is in season.

Rhubarb oatmeal crumble (see recipe) is deliciously crunchy — make Rhubarb and Madeira creams (see recipe) for the adults. Fresh fruit will go down well with adults and children alike, but if you make a cherry crumble, indulge the parents with Cherries flambéed with kirsch (see page 29). Rice pudding is another nursery favourite and can be simply adapted to make a peach condé for the adults: chill the rice pudding, then serve

it with peach halves and a sauce of melted redcurrant jelly mixed with lemon juice. Children will enjoy crêpes spread with jam or covered with lemon and sugar; crêpes Suzette are ideal for grown-up tastes.

Whichever dishes you choose for the two dinners, try to co-ordinate your cooking as much as possible. Prepare what you can in advance, particularly for the adults' dinner, so that once the children are fed and in bed or otherwise occupied you can sit down and have a drink before dinner.

Tomato-painted chicken legs

These coated chicken legs are bound to be a great favourite with children.

1 hour

Boiled or sautéed new potatoes

Serves 4
45 ml /3 tbls tomato ketchup
15 ml /1 tbls olive oil
1.5 ml /¼ tsp salt
4 chicken legs
cucumber relish, peas and Boiled or sautéed new potatoes, to serve (see recipe)

1 Heat the oven to 190C /375F /gas 5.
2 In a bowl, mix the tomato ketchup with the oil and salt.
3 Brush the chicken legs with the tomato ketchup mixture. Put them in a roasting tin and cook for 40–45 minutes or until the juices run clear when the thickest part of the leg is pierced.
4 Serve with cucumber relish, peas and Boiled or sautéed new potatoes.

● If you wish to serve this with chips, try using frozen or oven-cooked chips.

Chicken turnovers

 1¼ hours

Serves 4
4 chicken breasts, boned and skinned
600 ml /1 pt chicken stock, home-made or
from a cube
25 g /1 oz butter
225 g /8 oz button mushrooms, thinly sliced
salt and freshly ground black pepper
1.5 ml /¼ tsp allspice
30 ml /2 tbls coriander leaves, finely chopped
60 ml /4 tbls thick cream
flour, for dusting
225 g /8 oz made-weight puff pastry,
defrosted if frozen
a little milk
1 medium-sized egg, beaten
15 ml /1 tbls lemon juice
7.5 ml /½ tbls dry sherry
cooked asparagus tips, to garnish
cooked carrots, to garnish

1 Put the chicken breasts in a large shallow pan, cover with chicken stock and poach over a low heat until the breasts are white and firm but tender. Leave them to cool in the poaching liquid.
2 Melt the butter in a heavy-based saucepan over a moderate heat, add the mushrooms and cook for 10–15 minutes, stirring occasionally. Season with salt and black pepper, then mix in the allspice and coriander leaves. Leave to cool for 5 minutes.
3 Put the mushroom mixture in a blender, scraping all the pan sediments and adding them too. Pour in the cream and blend it all to a purée.
4 On a lightly floured board roll out the pastry to a rectangle with a thickness of just over 3 mm /⅛ in and cut it into 4.
5 Drain the chicken breasts and pat them dry on absorbent paper. Reserve the stock.
6 Put a chicken breast on each rectangle of pastry, placing it to one side.
7 Take half of the mushroom purée and spread some over each chicken breast in an even layer.
8 With a pastry brush, dampen the edges of the pastry with a little milk. Fold over the pastry, pressing down the edges with your fingertips to seal.
9 Brush the tops of the parcels with the beaten egg, taking care not to let it drip down the sides of the parcels.
10 Dampen a large baking sheet and put the pastry parcels on it. Refrigerate until needed or for at least 30 minutes.
11 Heat the oven to 220C /425F /gas 7.
12 Cook in the oven for 14–16 minutes or until well-risen and golden brown.
13 Meanwhile make the sauce; reduce the reserved chicken stock over a high heat until there is only 300 ml /10 fl oz. Add 60 ml /4 tbls of this to the remaining mushroom purée to thin it slightly, then add this to the stock in the pan and warm through.
14 Stir in the lemon juice and the sherry and bring to the boil. Let the sauce bubble for 1–2 minutes.

Chicken turnovers

15 Transfer the chicken turnovers from the baking sheet to a warmed serving dish, garnish with the asparagus tips and carrots and serve the sauce separately.

Boiled or sautéed new potatoes

 40 minutes

Serves 8
900 g /2 lb small new potatoes, approximately
60 in all
coarse salt
75–100 g /3–4 oz butter
finely chopped fresh parsley, to garnish

1 Wash the potatoes and either scrape or, if they peel easily, simply rub off the skins.
2 Put the potatoes in a pan. Cover with cold water, add a generous amount of salt and bring to the boil.
3 Simmer the potatoes until they feel soft when pierced with a fork. The small ones will take about 18 minutes.
4 Drain well and serve with plenty of butter and coarse salt to taste. Garnish with finely chopped parsley.

● Instead of removing all the skin from the potatoes, simply scrape or rub off a neat band of skin around the middle of each potato before boiling. This way of presenting boiled new potatoes allows you to enjoy the maximum flavour and goodness.
● Although it may seem an unusual idea, I like to sauté new potatoes. Boil the potatoes as above, then drain and slice thickly. Sauté them in 75 g /3 oz butter over a high heat, stirring gently until the potato slices are crisp and golden brown on all sides. Butter is not usually used for sautéeing at a high heat like this, but I think it gives the potatoes a wonderful colour and flavour (watch out that the butter does not brown though). Always serve the sautéed potatoes immediately.
● Left-over cold boiled potatoes may also be sliced and sautéed in butter, or they make a delicious salad if diced and mixed with thick mayonnaise and snipped chives.

Surprise potatoes

 2 hours

Serves 4
4 large potatoes, scrubbed but not peeled
salt
500 g /1 lb topside or 500 g /1 lb lean mince
30 ml /2 tbls olive oil
1 onion, coarsely chopped
4 carrots, finely sliced
600 ml /1 pt beef stock, home-made or from
a cube
45 ml /3 tbls tomato purée
25 g /1 oz butter
100 g /4 oz Cheddar cheese, finely grated
For the beurre manié
7.5 ml /½ tbls flour
7.5 ml /½ tbls butter

1 Heat the oven to 200C /400F /gas 6.
2 Prick the potatoes all over with a fork, sprinkle the skins with salt and bake in the oven for 1½ hours or until done.
3 Meanwhile, put the topside, if using, through the mincer twice.
4 Put the olive oil in a large heavy-based saucepan over a moderate heat. Add the mince and brown for 3–4 minutes.
5 Add the onion and carrots and sauté gently for a further 10 minutes.
6 Pour in the stock, stir thoroughly and simmer for 1 hour. Stir in the tomato purée and season lightly with salt.
7 For the *beurre manié*: mix together the flour and butter in a bowl. Roll it into small balls, then add to the mince mixture, a little at a time, stirring until thick. Simmer for another 10 minutes, stirring occasionally. Keep warm.
8 When the potatoes are cooked, cut them in half lengthways and scoop out all the potato, being careful not to pierce the skins.
9 Arrange the potato skins in a shallow, flameproof dish and fill with the mince stew.
10 Mash the potato with the butter until smooth, then pile on top of the mince-filled halves. Heat the grill to medium-high.
11 Sprinkle Cheddar cheese over each potato half, then grill for 5–10 minutes or until lightly browned. Serve immediately.

● As this recipe stands it is suitable for children and adults, but if you want to make it extra special, try including wine with the stock, or try adding a crushed clove of garlic to the meat.

Glazed peas

 10–15 minutes

Serves 4
500 g /1 lb frozen peas
50 g /2 oz butter
60 ml /4 tbls chicken stock, home-made or
from a cube
salt
freshly ground black pepper
4 leaves from the centre of a lettuce
15 ml /1 tbls lemon juice

1 Place the peas in a small saucepan. Add just enough cold water to cover and bring to the boil. Remove from the heat and drain.
2 Return the peas to the saucepan. Add the butter and the chicken stock, season with salt and pepper, half-covered, until nearly all the liquid is absorbed and the peas are tender — about 10 minutes.
3 Serve the peas piled in the lettuce leaves. Boil the pan juices with a little lemon juice to reduce them further and spoon a small amount over each serving.

● To give the peas extra flavour you can add 2 spring onions, finely chopped, to the simmering peas.
● Try using fresh peas, when available. To get 500 g /1 lb of shelled peas you will need 2 kg /4 lb of peas in the pod. Bring them to the boil and cook for 10 minutes, then proceed with the recipe.

Glazed peas

Rhubarb oatmeal crumble

Rhubarb crumble is always a family favourite — in this recipe the addition of oatmeal to the topping gives extra crunchiness. See my suggestions at the end of the recipe for differently flavoured crumbles.

 1¼ hours

Serves 4
700 g /1½ lb rhubarb
25 g /1 oz caster sugar
15 ml /1 tbls orange juice
thick cream, chilled, or vanilla ice cream,
* to serve*
For the crumble
125 g /4 oz flour
50 g /2 oz butter
40 g /1½ oz caster sugar
45 ml /3 tbls medium oatmeal
15 g /½ oz Demerara sugar

1 Top, tail and wash the rhubarb. Cut it into 25 mm /1 in lengths and put it into a 1.3 L /2¼ pt ovenproof dish. Sprinkle with the caster sugar and orange juice.

2 Heat the oven to 200C /400F /gas 6.
3 To make the crumble, put the flour into a large bowl, add the butter and caster sugar and mix lightly with your fingertips until the mixture resembles fine breadcrumbs.
4 Sprinkle the crumble mixture over the rhubarb.
5 Mix together the oatmeal and Demerara sugar and sprinkle over the crumble mixture.
6 Put the dish in the oven and bake for 45 minutes until the crumble is golden brown. Serve it immediately with chilled thick cream or a rich vanilla ice cream.

● Ginger crumble: fry 225 g /8 oz crushed ginger snaps in 75 g /3 oz butter.
● Nut crumble: fry 125 g /4 oz breadcrumbs, 50 g /2 oz mixed chopped nuts and 50 g /2 oz Demerara sugar in 50 g /2 oz butter.

Rhubarb and Madeira creams

Use rhubarb not only for the children's crumble but also for this sophisticated adult dessert flavoured with Madeira and lemon juice; it's delicious.

 1 hour, plus chilling

Serves 4
500 g /1 lb rhubarb
125 g /4 oz caster sugar
grated zest of 1 orange
1 large dessert apple
300 ml /10 fl oz thick cream
15 ml /1 tbls lemon juice
45 ml /3 tbls Madeira
1.5 ml /¼ tsp powdered cinnamon
ratafias, to serve

1 Heat the oven to 180C /350F /gas 4.
2 Top, tail and wash the rhubarb. Chop it into 25 mm /1 in lengths and put them in a shallow dish. Sprinkle with the sugar and grated orange zest, then cook for 35–40 minutes until the rhubarb is very soft. Leave to cool.
3 When the rhubarb is cool, put it in a blender together with its liquid.
4 Peel the apple and grate it into the blender. Blend the rhubarb and apple to a smooth purée.
5 Whip the cream in a large bowl until soft peaks form, then add the rhubarb and apple purée and stir well to mix.
6 Stir in the lemon juice, the Madeira and cinnamon, then pile the mixture into 4 individual serving glasses, and chill in the refrigerator for at least 3 hours.
7 Just before serving, put 2–3 ratafias in each glass so that they just dip into the creams. Serve immediately.

Time-Savers

INSTANT BREADS & SCONES

No-yeast breads and high-rise scones are quick to prepare and cook — you need spend no time waiting for the dough to rise. They can be plain, sweet or savoury and can help you if you run out of bread at any time.

No-yeast breads and scones give all the satisfaction of other home-made bread and cakes — freshness and a warm, welcoming smell straight from the oven. Yet they can be prepared and ready to cook, even without an electric food processor or mixer, in little more than 10 minutes. You can also give them an endless variety of flavours.

The basic ingredients are flour, salt and a raising agent instead of yeast. You can use self-raising flour which has sifted-in raising agents, but many cooks prefer to use plain flour and control precisely the amount of baking powder added. Scone, and some bread, recipes have a little added fat, butter or margarine, and they all have an acidic liquid that binds the dry ingredients together and forms a dough. Sour milk was traditionally used, but now, with modern milk sterilization processes, it is necessary to sour the milk by adding a little lemon juice to it or to use buttermilk, soured cream or yoghurt.

In scone recipes, where only a small quantity of liquid is needed, ring the changes by using fruit juice, which has the necessary amount of acid and gives a pleasant flavour variation (see Orange sugar scone). Some recipes require the addition of an egg. This gives a richer flavour, helps the rising process and adds protein. You need 1 egg for each 225 g /8 oz flour.

Try adding extra flavouring to plain bread or scones; caraway and seed breads go well with casseroles. Herb scones are excellent with soups or served with cheese and pickle.

Most no-yeast breads and scones are cooked in a hot oven, 220C /425F /gas 7. Keep the oven temperature constant, make up several batches of different types, one after another, and in a very short time you can make a large batch for the freezer.

For days when every second counts, you can make the bread or scone dough in advance and leave it shaped ready to bake. Wrap it in foil and keep it in the refrigerator, ready to pop into the oven when needed.

These breads and scones are so delicious that there is usually nothing left over. They are definitely at their best eaten on the day of baking — straight from the oven, or when they have cooled slightly. It is therefore better to freeze any extra, rather than keep them until the next day. If you do have some day-old bread or scones, restore them by placing them on a baking sheet, covering them with a cake tin and baking them on the bottom shelf of an oven at 140C /275F /gas 1 for 20 minutes. Cool the breads and scones on a wire rack.

Flavouring breads and scones
● For spiced bread, stir in 10 ml /2 tsp dry mustard, a pinch each of paprika and pepper.
● For herb bread, stir in 15 ml /1 tbls fresh herbs or 10 ml /2 tsp dried herbs after you have rubbed in the fats. You can use parsley, mint, marjoram, savory or basil — or make up your own mixture of herbs.
● For caraway bread, add 15 ml /1 tbls caraway seeds to the other dry ingredients.
● For honey bread, replace 45 ml /3 tbls of milk with the same amount of clear honey.
● For peanut bread, substitute 40 g /1½ oz peanut butter for the butter and stir in 50 g / 2 oz chopped salted peanuts.
● For tea-time, make the bread or scones sweet with the addition of sugar, honey, treacle, syrup or molasses. Add up to 50 g / 2 oz to each 225 g /8 oz flour. If you add a liquid sweetener, use 45 ml /3 tbls and reduce the amount of milk or yoghurt used accordingly.
● Make them sweeter and tastier with the addition of dried fruits. Add up to 100 g / 4 oz to each 225 g /8 oz flour. To make them more cake-like, sift 10 ml /2 tsp ginger, cinnamon, or mixed spice into the flour.

Freezing breads and scones
As soon as the breads and scones are cold pack them in heavy-duty polythene bags, seal, label and freeze for up to 6 months. When needed, defrost them in a low oven for 10–20 minutes.

Quick soda bread

Use part white and part wholemeal flour and enrich the recipe with an egg for a light and moist bread.

⏱ 35 minutes,
plus cooling

Makes an 18 cm /7 in round loaf
*25 g /1 oz butter, cut in dice, plus extra
   for greasing*
225 g /8 oz flour, plus extra for dusting
100 g /4 oz wholemeal flour
5 ml /1 tsp bicarbonate of soda
5 ml /1 tsp salt
10 ml /2 tsp caster sugar
1 medium-sized egg
150 ml /5 fl oz milk
5 ml /1 tsp lemon juice

1 Heat the oven to 220C /425F /gas 7. Grease and flour a baking sheet.
2 Sift the flours, soda, salt and sugar together in a bowl.
3 Rub in the butter until the mixture resembles fine breadcrumbs. Beat together the egg, milk and lemon juice and stir this into the dry ingredients. Mix them all into a soft dough.
4 Shape the dough into a ball and place it on the baking sheet. Slightly flatten it and mark a cross on the top.
5 Bake it for 25 minutes or until the bread sounds hollow when tapped on the underside. Cool on a wire rack.

Orange sugar scone

⏱ 25 minutes,
plus cooling

Makes 8 slices
*50 g /2 oz butter, cut in dice, plus extra for
   greasing*
*225 g /8 oz self-raising flour, plus extra for
   dusting*
25 g /1 oz caster sugar
grated zest of 1 orange
1 medium-sized egg
60 ml /4 tbls orange juice
For the topping
30 ml /2 tbls sugar
grated zest of ½ orange
butter and honey, to serve

1 Heat the oven to 220C /425F /gas 7. Grease and then flour a 20 cm /8 in round cake tin.
2 In a bowl, mix together the flour, caster sugar and orange zest. Rub in the butter until the mixture resembles fine breadcrumbs. Stir in the egg and orange juice and mix until a soft dough is formed. Knead the dough in the bowl until it is smooth.
3 Place the dough in the tin to cover the base evenly. Smooth over the top.
4 Mix the sugar and grated orange zest and sprinkle it over the top of the dough.
5 Bake it for 15 minutes, then remove the tin and stand it on a wire rack to cool for about 5–10 minutes. Slice the scone and serve warm, spread with butter and honey.

Cheese baps and Apricot spice scone

Tea-time scones

25 minutes,
plus cooling

Makes 8 scones
50 g /2 oz butter, plus extra for greasing
225 g /8 oz self-raising flour, plus extra for
  dusting
5 ml /1 tsp bicarbonate of soda
2.5 ml /½ tsp salt
150 ml /5 fl oz milk, plus extra for brushing
a few drops of lemon juice

1 Heat the oven to 220C /425F /gas 7.
Grease and flour a baking sheet.
2 In a bowl sift together the flour, soda and
salt. Rub in the butter until the mixture
resembles fine breadcrumbs. Mix together
the milk and lemon juice and stir this into
the dry ingredients. Mix until a soft dough
has been formed and then knead it lightly.
3 Roll out the dough on a lightly floured
board to a thickness of 15 mm /½ in. Stamp
out circles with a 5 cm /2 in cutter. Gather
the trimmings together and form them into a
ball. Lightly roll out this dough and cut more
scones. Brush the tops with milk.
4 Transfer them to the baking sheet and
bake in the oven for 12–15 minutes, until the
scones are well-risen and sound hollow when
rapped. Cool them on a wire rack.

● For spiced scones, mix 5–10 ml /1–2 tsp
mixed spice with the caster sugar. Or use half
mixed spice and half ground ginger.

Apricot spice scone

40 minutes,
plus cooling

Makes 8 slices
50 g /2 oz butter, cut in dice, plus extra
  for greasing and serving
225 g /8 oz wholemeal flour, plus extra
  for dusting
5 ml /1 tsp bicarbonate of soda
5 ml /1 tsp mixed spice
2.5 ml /½ tsp ground ginger
2.5 ml /½ tsp salt
100 g /4 oz dried apricots, chopped
150 ml /5 fl oz yoghurt
For the topping
30 ml /2 tbls milk
30 ml /2 tbls Demerara sugar

1 Heat the oven to 220C /425F /gas 7.
Grease and flour a baking sheet.
2 Sift together the flour, soda, spices and
salt in a bowl. Rub in the butter until the
mixture resembles fine breadcrumbs. Stir in
the apricots. Add the yoghurt and mix until
the dough is firm, then knead it lightly until
it is smooth.
3 Shape the dough into a round about 23
cm /9 in across. Place it on the baking sheet
and mark it into 8 wedges. Brush the top of
the dough with milk and then sprinkle the
sugar over it.
4 Bake it in the oven for 25 minutes.
Transfer the scone to a wire rack to cool and
serve warm with plenty of butter.

Cheese baps

35 minutes,
plus cooling

Makes 8 baps
75 g /3 oz white vegetable fat, plus extra for
  greasing
450 g /1 lb wholemeal flour, plus extra for
  dusting
5 ml /1 tsp salt
10 ml /2 tsp bicarbonate of soda
5 ml /1 tsp dry mustard
175 g /6 oz Cheddar cheese, grated
300 ml /11 fl oz milk, plus extra for brushing
10 ml /2 tsp lemon juice
10 ml /2 tsp celery seeds, for topping

1 Heat the oven to 200C /400F /gas 6.
Grease and flour a baking sheet.
2 Sift together the flour, salt, soda and dry
mustard in a bowl. Rub in the fat and stir in
the cheese. Sour 300 ml /11 fl oz milk with
the lemon juice and stir it into the dry
ingredients to form a dough. Knead the
dough lightly in the bowl.
3 Divide the dough into 8 portions and
shape each one into a round. Place them on
the baking sheet and flatten the dough to 25
mm /1 in thick. Brush the tops of the baps
with the rest of the milk and sprinkle them
with celery seeds.
4 Bake in the oven for 25 minutes. Place on
a wire rack to cool slightly — serve warm.

DISHES IN UNDER AN HOUR

There are many occasions when you need to provide food within one hour of starting the preparations. Here are a few ideas for delicious starters, main courses and sweets which can be prepared in a limited time.

Whenever you have to produce a meal without any warning, you may well have no alternative but to turn to your store cupboard. Dishes like Ham in Madeira sauce, served with Baby sweetcorn with water chestnuts (see recipes) make imaginative use of store-cupboard ingredients.

However, if you want to prepare a main course quickly but have had enough warning to be able to plan ahead slightly, you do not need to rely totally on convenience foods. Fresh meat, poultry, fish and eggs can all be cooked in a short time to produce impressive and nutritious main courses. The accompanying vegetable, pasta or rice can be fitted in while the main dish is cooking. The trick is to be very organized and not to panic. In this way you can produce a substantial main course within an hour — my recipes for these prove the point.

With a substantial main course you generally do not need to worry about a starter or dessert. However, if you do require a starter or pudding, there are numerous dishes you can make quickly while the main course is bubbling away.

For starters, slices of smoked, pickled or soused fish are good served with soured cream and chives, or made into a cocktail with bottled dressing and chopped herbs. Or try the Salmon creams en croûte recipe on the next page which makes use of canned red salmon. Canned soups are improved with a dash of sherry or vermouth, swirls of cream or yoghurt, and sprinklings of orange or lemon zest or herbs. Vegetables can be chopped with cooked meat, canned fish or hard-boiled eggs, then tossed in a vinaigrette or creamy dressing; tomatoes sliced with cheese (Mozzarella is best) and coated with a thick herby dressing are quick and delicious. Canned beans like haricots, red kidney and cannellini, served chilled in a salad with meat or fish, are some of the best standby starters that there are.

For speedy desserts, nothing can beat fresh fruit — see my recipe for Sliced oranges. Soft fruit (raspberries, cherries, strawberries) looks very pretty in a glass bowl served with sweet crisp biscuits and lashings of sweetened whipped cream (add vanilla essence for instant crème Chantilly). Alternatively, a selection of cheeses with clusters of sweet juicy grapes looks just as appealing as any elaborately decorated dessert.

If you have some fresh cream and the odd drop of brandy or liqueur, there is no end to the number of desserts you can make. Process them in a blender with canned fruit for a tasty mousse. (You could substitute yoghurt for fresh cream if preferred.) For a prettier effect, layer whipped cream in tall goblets with fruit and crushed sweet biscuits, meringues or crunchy brown sugar.

Crab with artichoke hearts

 20 minutes

Serves 6 as a starter, or 4 as a main course
225 g /8 oz canned crabmeat, well drained
5 ml /1 tsp Dijon mustard
1.5 ml /¼ tsp cayenne pepper
120 ml /8 tbls thick cream
salt
freshly ground black pepper
450 g /1 lb canned artichoke hearts
2 medium-sized egg whites
30 ml /2 tbls grated Parmesan cheese

1 Put the drained crabmeat into a large bowl with the mustard, the cayenne pepper, the cream, the salt and the black pepper. Mix them together thoroughly.
2 Put the artichoke hearts, together with their liquid, into a small saucepan and bring them to the boil. Simmer them for 5 minutes over a medium heat to warm them through, then drain them and keep them warm in a shallow, heatproof serving dish.
3 Whisk the egg whites until they form stiff peaks, then fold them into the crab mixture. Heat the grill to high.
4 Pile the crab mixture in mounds on top of the artichoke hearts. Sprinkle them

Curried eggs with biriani rice

generously with the grated Parmesan cheese and then put them under the grill for 3–4 minutes, until they are golden.

Salmon creams en croûte

 40 minutes

Serves 6

25 g /1 oz butter
1 onion, finely chopped
15 ml /1 tbls flour
150 ml /5 fl oz milk
50 g /2 oz canned button mushrooms, drained and sliced
25 g /1 oz anchovy-stuffed olives, sliced
15 ml /1 tbls capers
freshly grated nutmeg
5 ml /1 tsp dillweed
5 ml /1 tsp lemon juice
salt
freshly ground black pepper
225 g /8 oz canned red salmon
6 slices from a small white loaf, 3 cm /1¼ in thick
oil, for deep frying
30 ml /2 tbls grated Parmesan or other hard cheese
snipped fresh dill, to garnish

1 Melt the butter in a heavy-based saucepan, add the onion and sauté for 5 minutes, until soft and golden.
2 Stir in the flour, then gradually add the milk. Stir until the mixture thickens, then add the mushrooms, anchovy-stuffed olives, capers, nutmeg, dillweed, lemon juice and salt and freshly ground black pepper. Stir thoroughly, add the salmon and stir again. Simmer gently for 10 minutes to let the flavours blend.
3 Hollow out the slices of bread to make a cavity in the middle of each, leaving an edge of about 5 mm /¼ in.
4 Heat the oil in a deep-fat fryer to 190C / 375F — at this temperature a 25mm /1 in cube of day-old white bread will brown in 50 seconds. Fry the croûtons, 2 at a time, for 3 minutes each, then drain them on absorbent paper and keep them warm while you fry the remaining ones.
5 Heat the grill to high. Divide the salmon mixture among the croûtons. Sprinkle with the Parmesan cheese and put under the grill for 3 minutes, until the cheese is melted and bubbly. Garnish with snipped fresh dill and serve immediately.

● As a variation, serve the salmon mixture in scallop shells or ramekins instead of croûtons, if you prefer.

Curried eggs with biriani rice

 50 minutes

Serves 4

8 medium-sized eggs
30 ml /2 tbls vegetable oil
1 onion, peeled and finely chopped
1 garlic clove, peeled and crushed
15 ml /1 tbls ground cumin or coriander
5 ml /1 tsp ground turmeric
2.5 ml /½ tsp chilli powder, or to taste
salt
4 large tomatoes
600 ml /1 pt chicken stock, home-made or from a cube

For the biriani rice

30 ml /2 tbls vegetable oil
225 g /8 oz Basmati, Patna or long-grain rice, rinsed and drained
5 ml /1 tsp ground cumin
2.5 ml /½ tsp ground turmeric
salt
750 ml /1¼ pt hot chicken stock, home-made or from stock cubes
225 g /8 oz frozen mixed vegetables
25 g /1 oz soft butter
freshly ground black pepper

1 Cook the eggs in boiling water for 8 minutes until just hard-boiled and reserve.
2 Meanwhile, heat the oil in a large heavy pan or flameproof casserole. Add the chopped onion, garlic, spices and salt to taste and fry gently for 5 minutes until the onion is soft and transparent.
3 Meanwhile blanch and skin the tomatoes and then chop. Add them to the pan and stir-fry them for a few minutes. Stir in the stock and bring to the boil. Lower the heat and simmer uncovered for 20 minutes, stirring occasionally.
4 Prepare the rice: heat the oil in a heavy pan, add the rice, spices and salt to taste and fry gently for 5 minutes, stirring constantly.
5 Pour in the second quantity of hot stock and the frozen vegetables, stir once, then cover and cook over a gentle heat for 20 minutes until the rice is tender.
6 Shell the hard-boiled eggs and add to the curry sauce. Cook for a further 20 minutes, spooning the sauce over the eggs from time to time so they become well coated.
7 When the rice is tender, fork in the soft butter and add salt and black pepper to taste. Arrange the rice around the edge of a warmed serving dish. Taste and adjust the seasoning of the sauce, then pour it, with the eggs, into centre of the rice. Serve immediately.

Sweet peppers with anchovies

🔪 20 minutes

Serves 4
450 g /1 lb canned sweet red peppers
   (4–6 peppers)
8–12 anchovy fillets, drained
2 garlic cloves, finely chopped
120–180 ml /8–12 tbls olive oil
40–50 g /1½–2 oz butter
salt and freshly ground black pepper
a green salad, to serve
French bread, to serve

1 Heat the grill to high. Drain the peppers then cut them in half. Place them, cavities up, in a shallow flameproof serving dish.
2 Into each half pepper place 1 anchovy fillet, a pinch of garlic, 15 ml /1 tbls oil and a dot of butter. Sprinkle with salt and pepper and put under the grill for 10 minutes.
3 Serve with the salad and French bread.

● This light lunch, supper or starter can also be made just as easily with skinned fresh red or green peppers.

Ham in Madeira sauce and Baby sweetcorn with water chestnuts

Ham in Madeira sauce

🔪 35 minutes

Serves 4
25 g /1 oz butter
1 onion, very finely chopped
15 ml /1 tbls Madeira or sherry
300 ml /10 fl oz chicken stock, home-made or
   from a cube
5 ml /1 tsp dillweed
2.5 ml /½ tsp Dijon mustard
salt and freshly ground black pepper
grated zest of 1 lemon
10 whole allspice berries, crushed
4 cloves, crushed
450 g /1 lb canned ham, in 4 thick slices
5 ml /1 tsp flour
hot canned flageolet beans, to serve

1 Melt the butter in a frying-pan and sauté the onion for 5 minutes. Add the Madeira or sherry and let it bubble for 2–3 minutes.
2 Add the stock, dillweed, mustard, salt and pepper, lemon zest, allspice and cloves. Bring quickly to the boil, then lower the heat. Add the ham slices to the pan, spooning the sauce over them, then simmer gently for 15 minutes.
3 Place the slices of ham on a warmed serving platter and keep warm. Add the flour to the sauce and simmer for 2–3 minutes, stirring, until it thickens. Adjust the seasoning if necessary, then pour it over the ham. Surround the ham with the heated and drained flageolet beans and serve at once.

Liver with orange

Serve this dish with tagliatelle and a crisp green salad.

🔪 40 minutes

Serves 4
450–500 g /1–1¼ lb lamb's liver, thinly sliced
15 ml /1 tbls flour
salt and freshly ground black pepper
40 g /1½ oz butter
30 ml /2 tbls vegetable oil
1 onion, peeled and finely sliced
30 ml /2 tbls ginger marmalade
75 ml /3 fl oz frozen, concentrated orange
   juice, defrosted
425 ml /15 fl oz chicken stock, home-made
   or from a cube
2 oranges, peeled and sliced into thin rings

1 Coat the liver in seasoned flour. Melt 25 g /1 oz butter in a frying-pan with half the oil. Add the liver and fry over a brisk heat for 5 minutes until browned on all sides,

tossing the liver constantly. Remove the liver with a slotted spoon and set aside.

2 Heat the remaining oil in the pan, add the onion and half the marmalade. Scrape up the sediment from the bottom of the pan with a wooden spoon, then fry the onion gently until lightly coloured.

3 Gradually stir the orange juice into the pan, then the chicken stock. Add salt and pepper to taste, bring to the boil and simmer for 10 minutes until thickened.

4 Return the liver to the pan and simmer gently for 5 minutes, spooning the sauce over the liver frequently.

5 During the last 5 minutes' cooking time, melt the remaining butter in a separate pan. Stir in the remaining marmalade, then add the orange slices. Fry over moderate heat until glazed on both sides.

6 Taste and adjust the seasoning of the orange sauce, then transfer the liver and sauce to a warmed serving platter. Arrange the orange slices on top and serve at once.

Chicken kebabs with peanut sauce

 50 minutes

Serves 4
4 large boneless chicken breasts, cut into
* bite-sized pieces*
225 g /8 oz back bacon, cut into bite-sized
* pieces*
juice of ½ lemon
2.5 ml /½ tsp garlic granules or dried
* minced garlic*
1.5 ml /¼ tsp cayenne pepper
oil, for greasing
For the peanut sauce
25 g /1 oz butter
1 onion, peeled and very finely chopped
60 ml /4 tbls crunchy peanut butter
30 ml /2 tbls soy sauce
a pinch of cayenne pepper

1 Put the chicken and bacon in a bowl with the lemon juice, garlic and cayenne pepper. Stir well to mix the ingredients, then thread the meats on oiled skewers, alternating the chicken with the bacon. Set them aside. Heat the grill to high.

2 Make the peanut sauce: melt the butter in a heavy pan, add the onion and fry gently until soft. Stir in the peanut butter and fry for a few minutes until dark and thick, then gradually stir in the soy sauce, 150 ml /5 fl oz water and the cayenne pepper. Simmer for about 10 minutes until the sauce becomes thick, stirring constantly.

3 Brush a little of the peanut sauce over one side of the kebabs, then place them under the grill with the coated side facing the heat. Grill for about 5 minutes until browned, then turn the kebabs and brush them with more sauce.

4 Continue turning the kebabs and coating them with sauce. Repeat until they are cooked on all sides, about 20 minutes.

5 Remove the kebabs from the grill. Scrape the sauce from the bottom of the pan, over the kebabs and serve at once.

Cod, spinach and cheese bake

 55 minutes

Serves 4
450 g /1 lb frozen whole leaf spinach
2.5 ml /½ tsp grated nutmeg
salt and freshly ground black pepper
50 g /2 oz butter
4 cod steaks or cutlets, defrosted if frozen
45 ml /3 tbls flour
300 ml /10 fl oz milk
175 g /6 oz mature Cheddar cheese, grated
crusty French bread, to serve

1 Put the frozen spinach in a heavy pan and heat gently until thawed, turning it over and breaking up any large frozen pieces.

2 Drain the spinach thoroughly, then return it to the pan and toss it over a brisk heat until thoroughly dry. Stir in half the nutmeg and salt and pepper to taste.

3 Heat the oven to 180C /350F /gas 4. Meanwhile, melt the butter in a frying-pan, add the fish and fry over moderate heat for 2–3 minutes on each side until the outside of the flesh turns white.

4 Place the spinach in the bottom of a baking dish. Remove the fish from the butter with a spatula, drain it thoroughly, then place it on top of the spinach and sprinkle with salt and pepper.

5 Pour the butter and fish juices from the frying-pan into the pan in which the spinach was thawed. Heat gently, then sprinkle in the flour and cook for 1 minute, stirring constantly. Remove it from the heat and gradually add the milk, beating vigorously after each addition.

6 Return the pan to the heat and bring to the boil. Lower the heat and simmer until thick, stirring constantly. Add 100 g /4 oz cheese, the remaining nutmeg and salt and pepper. Stir until the cheese has melted.

7 Pour the cheese sauce over the fish, then sprinkle with the remaining cheese. Bake for 30 minutes. Serve hot with French bread.

Sliced oranges

Baby sweetcorn with water chestnuts

 10 minutes

Serves 4
225 g /8 oz canned water chestnuts, drained
450 g /1 lb canned baby sweetcorn, drained
50 g /2 oz butter
15 ml /1 tbls brown sugar
5 ml /1 tsp dry sherry
salt and freshly ground black pepper

1 Cut the water chestnuts into thin slices, then combine them with the sweetcorn in a saucepan. Add the butter and melt over a low heat.

2 When the butter is melted, stir in the sugar and sherry and season to taste with salt and freshly ground black pepper. Let it simmer for 7–8 minutes until the butter has caramelized slightly. Transfer to a serving dish and serve immediately.

Sliced oranges

10 minutes,
plus chilling

Serves 4–6
3–4 large oranges
150 ml /5 fl oz fresh orange juice
30 ml /2 tbls caster sugar
275 ml /10 fl oz thick cream

1 Grate the zest of 1 orange and add to the orange juice. Peel all the oranges and cut off all the pith with a sharp knife. Cut the flesh into thin slices and remove the pips.

2 Place the orange slices in overlapping rows in a shallow serving dish, leaving the edges free. Sprinkle with orange juice, and half the caster sugar. Chill until needed.

3 Whip the thick cream and fold in the remaining caster sugar. Spoon the whipped cream and sugar onto the middle of the orange slices, making sure the edges of the slices are left free, to prevent the orange juice from mixing with the cream.

RECHAUFFEES

Small amounts of cooked meat, fish, poultry or vegetables are worth their weight in gold when you are looking for something to fill an omelette or jazz up a soufflé. But why not be more adventurous with your leftovers?

Many cooks only seriously consider using leftovers at Christmas-time or on other occasions when they have large amounts of food to prepare and guests who are tired of slices of cold meat or turkey.

But the wise and economical cook practises this art all year round, actually planning meals so that there is always something left. Small amounts of leftovers can be turned into ingenious starters and larger amounts into substantial supper or lunch dishes saving both time and money.

In this chapter I am going to concentrate on réchauffées. The name comes from the French word *réchauffer*, to reheat, and these are dishes which make the best use of planned leftovers.

Useful leftovers
Mince, chop or shred any leftover meat and vegetables to produce hashes, croquettes and patties, delicate steamed loaves and savoury sauces.

With left-over turkey, whether it be at Christmas-time or any other time of the year, try my American-inspired Turkey divan (see recipe) or the delicious Turkey ring mould (see recipe). For extra ideas on how to make the most of leftovers, see the information in my chapter on Using up left-over chicken (page 20).

Preparation
Cooked leftovers should be used up as soon as possible but storing them correctly will help to prolong their life. Cool the food as quickly as possible after it is cooked. If it is meat or poultry on the bone, remove it in neat chunks. As soon as it is cold, wrap the food in cling film or foil to prevent it drying out, and store it in the refrigerator until you are ready to use it.

For most réchauffée dishes the cooked ingredient is either minced, chopped or shredded; do this just before you are ready to use it. It is also best to trim off any excess fat as this does not taste very pleasant when re-heated.

Combining ingredients: it is better to have only one or at the most two cooked ingredients in any réchauffée dish although a number of different vegetables, of course, are acceptable together. Do not, however, make any dish a 'rag bag' of all your leftovers! By nature, leftovers are uniformly soft in texture; counteract this wherever possible with strips of raw or lightly cooked vegetables such as celery, peppers, mushrooms and chopped onions, or with nuts — any ingredient in fact, that has a good bite to its texture.

Give some thought to colour. Chopped tomatoes or canned red pimento, a few green peas or freshly chopped green herbs will all liven up the appearance of the finished dish. Remember also to season the dish well, as it

may be rather bland in flavour and in need of some 'livening up'.

Cooking the réchauffée
In principle a réchauffée is re-heated, rather than cooked, as the main ingredient is cooked already. However, the name should not be interpreted too literally. You may, for example, want to enclose your leftovers in a savoury custard, which needs time to cook.

Quick re-heating preserves as much of the goodness in the food as possible and also helps to keep it looking good. Slicing, mincing or cubing the food helps to speed up the re-heating process. It is a good idea to fold the ingredients into a sauce; this helps to keep the whole dish moist, gives it added flavour and makes the re-heating easier.

Salmon boreks

Filo pastry is available ready-made in sheets from good delicatessens. Once you have made up the pastry triangles, they can be stored in the refrigerator for up to 24 hours and cooked just before serving.

 cooking the salmon, then 1¾ hours

Makes 12
95 g /3½ oz butter
15 ml /1 tbls flour
30 ml /2 tbls milk
60 ml /4 tbls thick cream
15 ml /1 tbls finely chopped fresh chives
salt and freshly ground black pepper
lemon juice
175 g /6 oz cooked salmon, flaked
6 sheets of filo pastry

1   In a heavy-based saucepan, melt 15 g /½ oz of the butter and blend in the flour. Cook for 2–3 minutes, stirring, to form a pale roux; gradually stir in the milk, stirring with a wire whisk to prevent lumps forming, and add the thick cream. Bring to the boil, stirring constantly, add the finely chopped chives and season to taste with salt, freshly ground black pepper and lemon juice, to taste. Remove from the heat and stir in the flaked salmon. Allow to cool.
2   Heat the oven to 220C /425F /gas 7. Melt the remaining butter and use a little of it to brush a baking sheet.
3   To shape the boreks, cut each sheet of filo pastry in half. Brush one side of the half with melted butter. Place 15 ml /1 tbls of the cold salmon mixture in one corner, slightly off centre and 25 mm /1 in from the edge. Fold the sheet over so that it is halved lengthways again. You now have a long narrow strip of pastry. Brush with more melted butter. Take the short end, with the salmon filling, and fold it over to seal in the filling,

making a triangle shape. Then take the same end and fold it over itself. Continue folding the strip over and over onto itself, keeping it in the shape of a triangle. Tuck in the end neatly. Repeat with the remaining sheets of filo pastry and the fish mixture.
4   Arrange the triangles on the buttered baking sheet and brush the tops all over with more melted butter.
5   Bake the boreks in the oven for 10–15 minutes until they are puffed and golden.

Turkey ring mould

1 hour 10 minutes

Serves 4
15 g /½ oz butter, plus extra for greasing
350 g /12 oz cooked turkey
1 medium-sized onion, finely chopped
50 g /2 oz fresh white breadcrumbs
1 green pepper, finely diced
1 celery stick, finely diced
30 ml /2 tbls finely chopped fresh parsley
150 ml /5 fl oz milk
150 ml /5 fl oz turkey gravy or stock, or
   chicken stock made with a cube
2 eggs, beaten
4 ml /¾ tsp salt
freshly ground black pepper
For 225 ml /8 fl oz tomato sauce
25 g /1 oz butter
500 g /1 lb ripe tomatoes, skinned,
   seeded and finely chopped
30 ml /2 tbls tomato purée
125 ml /4 fl oz thick cream
salt
freshly ground black pepper

1   Heat the oven to 180C /350F /gas 4.
2   Butter a 1.1 L /2 pt plain ring mould and a square of foil to cover the top.
3   Dice the cooked turkey meat.
4   In a small pan, melt the butter, add the finely chopped onion and cook it gently, stirring occasionally, until soft and golden (5 minutes).
5   In a large bowl, add the sautéed onions to the diced turkey meat and the remaining ingredients and mix well.
6   Pack the mixture into the ring mould. Level off the top and cover it tightly with the buttered foil.
7   Stand the ring mould in a deep baking dish or roasting tin. Add enough boiling water to the tin to come two-thirds up the side of the mould.
8   Bake in the oven for 50 minutes, or until the mixture is firm to the touch.
9   Meanwhile, make the tomato sauce. Melt the butter in a frying-pan, add the chopped tomatoes and purée and cook, stirring constantly, for about 5 minutes or until smooth. Add the cream and season. Simmer, uncovered, for about 10 minutes, stirring occasionally until the sauce is slightly thickened. Taste and re-season it. Keep it hot.
10   When the mould is cooked, slip the tip of a knife around the sides of the mould and turn it out onto a heated dish. Pour over the sauce and serve.

Salmon boreks

Hot vegetable and bacon salad

 15 minutes

Serves 4–6
30 ml /2 tbls olive oil
175 g /6 oz bacon in one piece, diced
4 slices day-old bread, crusts removed, cut into
*   15 mm /½ in dice*
1 large garlic clove, finely chopped
350 g /12 oz cooked cauliflower florets
175 g /6 oz cooked mange tout
175 g /6 oz cooked green beans
salt
freshly ground black pepper
60 ml /4 tbls red wine vinegar

1   In a large frying-pan, heat the olive oil and sauté the diced bacon until golden. Remove with a slotted spoon and drain on absorbent paper and keep warm.
2   Fry the diced bread until golden brown on all sides, adding more oil if necessary and tossing with a spatula. Remove with a slotted spoon, drain on absorbent paper and keep warm with the bacon.
3   Add the finely chopped garlic to the pan and cook for 1 minute or until softened. Add the cooked cauliflower florets and cook for 1–2 minutes or until warmed through. Add the mange tout and green beans and cook for a further 1 minute until warmed through.

4   Season with salt and freshly ground black pepper to taste and add the sautéed bacon and the croûtons. When everything is very hot, pour over the vinegar, toss lightly, transfer to a warmed serving dish and then serve the salad immediately.

Soured cream veal

 45 minutes

Serves 6
18 button onions
300 ml /10 fl oz thick cream
juice of 1 lemon
45 ml /3 tbls finely chopped fresh chives
salt
freshly ground black pepper
6 slices of roast veal
paprika

1   Heat the oven to 170C /325F /gas 3.
2   Place the onions in boiling water for 1 minute. Remove with a slotted spoon and peel off the skins.
3   In a saucepan, bring the thick cream to just below boiling point, add the button onions, lemon juice and chopped chives. Season to taste.
4   Lay the slices of veal, overlapping, in a shallow ovenproof dish. Pour over the hot sauce and cook in the oven for 20 minutes. Transfer to a heated serving dish and sprinkle with paprika. Serve immediately.

Soured cream veal and Hot vegetable and bacon salad

Tasty meat filling

This is a good, meaty filling for ravioli or cannelloni and can also make a main-course dish. This recipe is enough to fill 4 servings of ravioli; make 3 times the quantity for 4 servings of cannelloni.

 10 minutes

Makes 180 ml /12 tbls
15 g /½ oz butter
7.5 ml /1½ tsp olive oil
125 g /4 oz cooked beef, minced
50 g /2 oz cooked veal, minced
15 ml /1 tbls fresh white breadcrumbs
15 ml /1 tbls freshly grated Parmesan cheese
10 ml /2 tsp finely chopped fresh parsley
1 egg
15 ml /1 tbls strong beef stock, home-made or
*   from a cube, plus extra if mixture is dry*
10 ml /2 tsp tomato purée
a pinch of ground cinnamon
salt and freshly ground black pepper

1   Heat the butter and olive oil in a heavy frying-pan or saucepan and sauté the minced meats for 5 minutes, stirring and tossing them with a fork to break them up so they cook on all sides. Remove from the heat.
2   Stir in the breadcrumbs, freshly grated

Parmesan cheese and chopped fresh parsley.
3 In a bowl, beat the egg with 15 ml /1 tbls beef stock and the tomato purée. Stir this into the meat mixture. Add the cinnamon and season with salt and pepper. The mixture should be moist and malleable; if it is not, add more beef stock. Allow the filling to become cold before using.

Danish delight

boiling and cooling the potatoes, then 45 minutes

Serves 6
500 g /1 lb cooked, cold lean beef, lamb, pork or bacon
2 onions
6 cooked new potatoes, in their skins
50 g /2 oz butter
salt
freshly ground black pepper
Worcestershire sauce, to season
6 medium-sized eggs
parsley sprigs, to garnish

1 Cut the meat into 10 mm /½ in cubes and reserve. Cut the onions and potatoes into pieces the same size as the meat and reserve them separately.
2 Melt one-third of the butter in a large frying-pan over a medium heat. When it is hot, sauté the meat for 4 minutes, stirring occasionally. Remove the meat from the pan and keep it warm. Repeat with the onions and then the potatoes.
3 Mix the meat, onions and potatoes together in the frying-pan and cook them for a further 5 minutes, stirring occasionally. Season to taste with salt, pepper and Worcestershire sauce. Pile the mixture onto a heated serving dish and reserve.
4 Meanwhile fry the eggs. Put them on top of the sautéed mixture, garnish and serve.

Ham hash

This is a simple dish to cook and it is always popular at suppertime.

45 minutes

Serves 2
550 g /1¼ lb floury potatoes
salt
225 g /8 oz freshly cooked ham
1 medium-sized onion, quartered
1 green pepper, seeded and cored
freshly ground black pepper
2.5 ml /½ tsp dried thyme
30 ml /2 tbls olive oil
15 g /½ oz butter

1 Boil the potatoes in salted water until tender. Drain them thoroughly and toss them in the dry pan over a moderate heat to evaporate any excess moisture.
2 Put the cooked potatoes, cooked ham, raw onion and green pepper through the coarsest blade of your mincer, or very finely chop them up together. Season to taste with salt and freshly ground black pepper, then add the dried thyme and mix well together.
3 Heat the olive oil in a heavy-based 20 cm / 8 in frying-pan. Add the hash mixture; shape it into an even cake with a spatula or the back of a spoon, and cook over a moderate heat for 5 minutes, or until the cake is crisp and golden underneath. Meanwhile, heat the grill to high.
4 Dot the butter on top of the ham hash and put it under the grill for 3–4 minutes or until the top is well browned. Serve immediately, cut into thick wedges.

Turkey divan

1 hour

Serves 4
350 g /12 oz cooked turkey
250 g /9 oz frozen broccoli, cooked
60 ml /4 tbls freshly grated Parmesan cheese
For the cream sauce
300 ml /10 fl oz milk
45 g /1½ oz butter
45 ml /3 tbls flour
1 chicken stock cube
freshly ground black pepper
150 ml /5 fl oz thick cream
30–45 ml /2–3 tbls dry sherry
2 egg yolks
salt

Danish delight

1 Heat the oven to 180C /350F /gas 4.
2 Cut the cooked turkey into small slices or cubes.
3 Drain the cooked broccoli thoroughly and arrange it neatly over the base of a 1.1 L / 2 pt ovenproof oval dish. Sprinkle the broccoli with 30 ml /2 tbls of the freshly grated Parmesan cheese.
4 To make the cream sauce, bring the milk to the boil in a saucepan. In another saucepan, melt the butter, blend in the flour and cook over a low heat for 2–3 minutes to make a pale roux, stirring constantly.
5 Gradually add the hot milk, stirring vigorously to prevent any lumps forming. Crumble in the chicken stock cube and a little freshly ground black pepper; bring it to the boil and simmer very gently, stirring slowly, for 2–3 minutes or until the sauce has thickened.
6 Stir in the thick cream. Bring the sauce to just below boiling point (do not boil it or the cream may curdle) and remove it from the heat.
7 Beat in the sherry and the egg yolks. Season with salt and freshly ground black pepper to taste.
8 Spoon half the sauce over the broccoli. Arrange the sliced or cubed turkey on the top and cover with the remaining sauce. Sprinkle with the remaining grated Parmesan cheese over the sauce.
9 Bake for 30 minutes in the oven, or until the dish is hot all through and the sauce is bubbling and golden brown on the top.

COOK-AHEAD WEEKEND MEALS

If you have guests to stay at the weekend, catering for them can be quite a job, but do not let the thought of all the extra cooking spoil the occasion for you. With a little careful planning all should go smoothly.

To help you entertain at the weekend with the minimum of fuss, here are two menus which, despite their sophistication, are extremely convenient to make. Bearing in mind that you will prefer to spend your time with your family and friends rather than alone in the kitchen, I have put together dishes which either take little time to make or which can be prepared ahead and then completed very simply.

If you want to start cooking a couple of weeks ahead there are several recipes in the chapter Making the most of your freezer (see page 70) which could be of some help. There is a basic beef recipe which can be transformed into three other dishes — Red beef casserole, Orange, beef and celery casserole or Hazelnut, beef and tomato casserole, all made from the same starting point! There are also suggestions for preparing varied and separate dishes with pork fillet.

Cook-ahead meal for 6
Start with Parma ham and fresh figs, an easy appetizer which only takes 10 minutes to prepare. For the main course, a casserole is the obvious answer. My Poule au pot à la bearnaise is a wonderful chicken dish from South-west France.

As a bonus, the stock is well worth serving as a soup course in its own right. In particular, it makes an ideal alternative starter for children and young people who have not yet acquired a taste for such ingredients as Parma ham and figs.

For dessert, offer Alsatian almond tart, impressive and delicious. It can be completed in advance and chilled until needed, then popped into the oven for half an hour before the meal. To drink, I suggest a Vin de Cahors red wine, which also comes from South-west France.

Planning the meal for 6
At least two days before the meal write out a check list of everything that you will need and then compose a comprehensive shopping list. Try to get all the purchases you will require in one shopping expedition — this will save an enormous amount of time and trouble. Try to prepare and chill the Alsatian tart as well.

The next day, begin the preparations for the Poule au pot à la bearnaise by simmering the chicken. You can also stuff the cabbage leaves, which is a fiddly and time-consuming job and so best not left until the last minute, when you will probably have more than enough other things to attend to. Prepare the casserole and then chill this in the refrigerator.

Poule au pot à la bearnaise

On the day of the meal very little will need to be done until an hour or so before the meal is to be served. Prepare and chill the Parma ham with fresh figs and put it in the refrigerator until required. Simmer the stuffed cabbage leaves, then add the turnips and the rest of the cabbage to the casserole which should be gently heating and needing little attention.

This is the time to spoon the jam into your Alsatian tart and then bake it in the oven, so that it has an opportunity to cool before you serve it.

If you have some guests who prefer to have the delicious soup instead of the Parma ham with fresh figs, then remember that you need to transfer the chicken to a heated serving dish and keep it hot until the time to carve. Then you can serve the soup with just a sprinkling of fresh parsley as a garnish for those who want it.

Cook-ahead meal for 8
Smoked trout mayonnaise is a convenient appetizer; it can be prepared ahead, with only minimal finishing needed on the day.

Follow this tasty starter with another dish requiring very little last-minute attention. My Casseroled pork has a very good, strong rich flavour which will develop further if it has been cooked a day ahead, left to mature and then gently reheated. Serve it with Buttered leeks with chives and make life a little easier for yourself by slicing and washing the leeks the day before they are needed and leaving them, covered, in the refrigerator until they are required. Remember, too, to prepare the clarified butter in advance.

Strawberry flan chantilly is a wonderful dessert. Make the flan case ahead and fill it at the very last minute with strawberries and a luscious crème chantilly.

The wine to offer with this menu is a St Emilion — a good red claret which will complement the Casseroled pork and the vegetables beautifully.

Planning the meal for 8
Again, I suggest that a few days before the actual event, you should make a check list of everything needed, sort out a shopping list and get the shopping done as soon as possible.

The pastry for the Strawberry flan chantilly can be made at leisure and cooked and stored in an airtight tin. The Casseroled pork, the Smoked trout mayonnaise and the Buttered leeks with chives can all be prepared the day before which will leave you little to do until half an hour before the meal when the casserole can be gently heated, the appetizer assembled and the fruit for the Strawberry flan chantilly macerated.

MEAL FOR 6

Here is the menu for your weekend meal to feed 6 people.

Parma ham with fresh figs

10 minutes,
then 1 hour chilling

Serves 6
6 fresh figs
6 thin slices Parma ham
To serve
freshly ground black pepper
freshly ground coriander seeds

1 Peel the figs very carefully and then cut them in half lengthways.
2 Roll each slice of ham into a cornet. Reserving 6 fig halves, fill each ham cornet with one of the remaining fig halves.
3 Arrange the cornets and the reserved fig halves, cut-side up, on a serving dish.
4 Chill the appetizer until you are ready to serve it. Serve it together with the freshly ground pepper and coriander seeds.

● You could serve Parma ham with honey-dew melon — a classic Italian hors d'oeuvre.

Poule au pot à la bearnaise

1½ hours and cooling,
then 40 minutes

Serves 6
2.3 kg /5 lb chicken
bouquet garni
1 small onion, stuck with 2 cloves
1 garlic clove, finely chopped
4 carrots, peeled and halved
2 leeks, white part only
1 celery stick
salt and freshly ground black pepper
1 kg /2 lb green cabbage
3 small turnips, peeled and halved
For the stuffing
1 chicken liver, minced
75 g /3 oz lean minced veal or chicken
50 g /2 oz ham, minced
75 g /3 oz streaky bacon, minced
15 g /½ oz butter
1 medium-sized onion, finely chopped
75 g /3 oz fresh white breadcrumbs
milk
15 ml /1 tbls finely chopped fresh parsley
15 ml /1 tbls brandy
a pinch of ground allspice
1 small egg, beaten
25 ml /1 fl oz thick cream
salt and freshly ground black pepper

1 Wipe the chicken inside and out with a damp cloth. Place it in a large saucepan or flameproof casserole and cover it with 1.7 L / 3 pt cold water. Add the bouquet garni, the onion stuck with cloves, the finely chopped garlic, the halved carrots, the leeks and the celery. Bring the ingredients to the boil, then season them generously with salt and freshly ground black pepper. Next, reduce the heat, cover and simmer gently for 1¼ hours, or until the chicken is nearly cooked. Take the chicken from the oven and leave it to get cold, then chill it in the pan.
2 Meanwhile, prepare the stuffing. In a bowl, combine the minced chicken liver with the veal or chicken, the ham and the minced streaky bacon.
3 In a small saucepan, heat the butter over a medium heat and then sauté the finely chopped onion for 7–10 minutes, or until it is softened, stirring occasionally. Leave the onion to get cold.
4 In a clean bowl, soak the breadcrumbs in milk. Squeeze out the excess moisture, then add the breadcrumbs to the minced meats with the cooled sautéed onion, the finely chopped parsley, brandy, a pinch of allspice, the beaten egg and the thick cream. Season the mixture generously with salt and freshly ground black pepper.
5 Next, prepare the cabbage. Bring a large saucepan of salted water to the boil. Plunge in the cabbage, head downwards, then cover and simmer it for 7 minutes, or until the

Parma ham with fresh figs

outer leaves are tender but still crisp. Drain the cabbage thoroughly and remove 12 large outer leaves. Drain them well on absorbent paper.

6 Divide the stuffing among the leaves, spooning it neatly into the centre. Next, fold over the sides of each leaf and roll up, tying each package with string. Cover them with cling film and chill. Cover the remaining cabbage and chill it also.

7 About 40 minutes before serving, place the saucepan with the chicken over a moderate heat and bring it to the boil. Add the cabbage parcels and then simmer for 10 minutes.

8 In the meantime, quarter the remaining cabbage and add it to the chicken together with the prepared turnips. Cook for 20–30 minutes.

9 To serve, remove the cabbage and stuffing rolls with a slotted spoon. Arrange them on a large warm serving dish. Drain the chicken, reserving the stock for further use, if wished, and place the cooked bird in the centre of the serving dish and surround it with the remaining vegetables.

Alsatian almond tart

30 minutes, plus chilling for the pastry, then 30 minutes, plus cooling

Serves 6
100 g /4 oz butter, plus extra for greasing
1 egg
225 g /8 oz caster sugar
225 g /8 oz flour, plus extra for dusting
225 g /8 oz ground almonds
120 ml /8 tbls raspberry jam

1 Lightly butter a baking sheet.
2 In a bowl, combine the egg and sugar. Beat them hard until they become pale and light.
3 Put the butter in a small saucepan and melt it over a gentle heat. Leave the butter until it is lukewarm but still liquid, then gradually beat it into the egg and sugar mixture. Beat this thoroughly for 2–3 minutes.
4 Sift the flour over the mixture, then beat it in. Sprinkle over the ground almonds, then beat these in. If the paste is too thick in consistency, add 15–30 ml /1–2 tbls water and blend in well.
5 On a lightly floured board, roll out the paste until it is about 15 mm /½ in thick.

Alsatian almond tart

Cut a 22.5 cm /9 in round and reserve the trimmings. Carefully transfer the round to the prepared baking sheet.
6 Roll out the pastry trimmings and then cut them into thin ribbons. Position one or several ribbons around the edge of the circle of pastry. Arrange the remaining ribbons in a trellis pattern over the top.
7 Using a teaspoon, carefully spoon the raspberry jam into the gaps between the strips of pastry. Cover the tart with cling film and then refrigerate it until you are ready to bake it.
8 To serve, heat the oven to 180C /350F / gas 4. Bake the tart for 25–30 minutes, or until it is a pale golden brown.
9 Remove it from the oven. Leave it to cool until it is lukewarm before serving.

● Serve the tart with thick whipped cream, if wished.
● As a variation, any flavour of jam may be used to fill the tart.

MEAL FOR 8

Here are the recipes for your weekend meal for 8 people.

Smoked trout mayonnaise

🍴 40 minutes preparation,
then 5 minutes finishing

Serves 8
4 × 225 g /8 oz smoked trout
100 g /4 oz green pepper, halved, seeded and finely chopped
6 spring onions, green parts only, chopped
120 ml /8 tbls mayonnaise
salt and freshly ground black pepper
8 crisp lettuce leaves
8 sprigs of watercress, to garnish
2 large tomatoes, to garnish
cayenne pepper

1 Skin the trout. Cut off the head and tail from each fish, then slit the skin down the centre of the back. Slit the skin down the other side, along the belly. Lift the skin with the point of the knife and peel it away with your fingers. Turn the fish over and remove the remaining skin in the same way. Cut through the flesh along the centre of the belly and open to expose the backbone. Lift out the backbone and scrape away any remaining dark skin and bone. Dice the flesh.
2 In a bowl, combine the diced trout, the green pepper and the spring onions. Add the mayonnaise and toss to coat. Season to taste.

Smoked trout mayonnaise

Cover and chill. Wrap the lettuce and watercress in a clean tea-towel and chill.
3 Just before serving, cut each tomato into 8 wedges. Put a lettuce leaf on each of 8 plates, hollow side up, and divide the trout mixture evenly among the leaves. Garnish each serving with tomato wedges and watercress. Dust with cayenne pepper and serve.

Casseroled pork

🍴 ahead: about 2 hours
to serve: 20 minutes reheating

Serves 8
1.8 kg /4 lb boned shoulder of pork
60 ml /4 tbls flour
salt and freshly ground black pepper
finely grated zest of ½ lemon
30 ml /2 tbls olive oil
25 g /1 oz butter
3 Spanish onions, finely chopped
2 garlic cloves, finely chopped
6 carrots, sliced
225 g /8 oz lean sliced bacon, cut in strips
bouquet garni
piece of orange zest
5 ml /1 tsp dried thyme
1 bay leaf
150 ml /5 fl oz red wine
425 ml /15 fl oz beef stock, home-made or from a cube
30 ml /2 tbls finely chopped fresh herbs

1 Cut the pork into 25 mm /1 in cubes, discarding any fat or gristle.
2 Spread the flour in a shallow container and season to taste with salt and freshly ground black pepper, and with the finely grated lemon zest. Toss the pork cubes in the seasoned flour until they are well coated.

3 In a large flameproof casserole, heat the olive oil and butter. When the foaming subsides, add enough pork to cover the base of the casserole and sauté it until it is golden brown on all sides. Remove to a plate using a slotted spoon and repeat until all the pork is browned.
4 Add the chopped onions and garlic and sauté, stirring from time to time with a wooden spoon, for 15 minutes, or until the onions are soft but not coloured.
5 Add the pork, the sliced carrots and the strips of bacon, the bouquet garni and the orange zest, the dried thyme and the bay leaf. Continue to cook.
6 Meanwhile, in a saucepan, combine the red wine and the stock and bring it to the boil. Pour this over the meat and bring it back to the boil. Skim off any scum that rises.
7 Reduce the heat, cover and simmer gently for 1¼ hours, or until the meat is tender. Leave it to cool if you are not going to serve it immediately. Chill it if you are not serving it on the same day.
8 To serve, reheat if necessary, adjust the seasoning, sprinkle with finely chopped herbs and serve from the casserole.

Buttered leeks with chives

🍴 clarifying the butter,
then 20–25 minutes

Serves 8
10 medium-sized leeks
150 ml /5 fl oz clarified butter (see below)
salt and freshly ground black pepper
60 ml /4 tbls finely snipped fresh chives

1 Cut off and discard the roots and the tough part of the green tops. Slice the leeks into 5 mm /¼ in circles. Put the circles in a colander and rinse them very thoroughly under cold running water to remove any grit and dirt. Drain the leeks well.
2 In a large frying-pan, heat the clarified butter and add the drained leek circles. Cover them and then sauté them over a moderate heat for 3 minutes. Turn the leeks carefully with a spatula, keeping the circles whole.
3 Cover the frying-pan again and sauté for a further 3 minutes, or until the leeks are tender but not too soft in texture. Season the vegetables to taste with salt and freshly ground black pepper.
4 Transfer the leek circles to a heated serving platter. Sprinkle them with the finely snipped chives and then serve them as soon as possible.

● To make clarified butter, put 225 g /8 oz butter in a small heavy-based saucepan and then melt it very gently. The foam from the butter will fall gently to the bottom of the pan, leaving the clarified butter as clear as oil on the top. Pour this into a bowl very carefully, without disturbing the white sediment. Keep the clarified butter in the refrigerator and use it as needed.

Buttered leeks with chives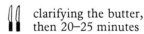

Strawberry flan chantilly

 making the pastry case,
then 30 minutes

Serves 8
600 g /1¼ lb strawberries
90 ml /6 tbls Grand Marnier
45–60 ml /3–4 tbls caster sugar
350 ml /12 fl oz thick cream
1 egg white
25 cm /10 in shortcrust pastry case,
  fully baked blind
10 ml /2 tsp ground cinnamon

To decorate
8 whole strawberries
8 fresh mint leaves

1 Hull 600 g /1¼ lb strawberries and slice them into a bowl. Pour over the Grand Marnier and sprinkle with 45–60 ml /3–4 tbls caster sugar to taste. Stir to mix and then leave the fruit to macerate in the refrigerator for at least 30 minutes.
2 In a bowl, whip the cream until thick. In a separate bowl, whisk the egg white until stiff but not dry, then fold it into the whipped cream. Refrigerate the mixture until ready to serve.
3 Just before serving, sprinkle the pastry case lightly with ground cinnamon.

4 Remove the strawberries from the liquid with a slotted spoon and spread them on the base of the flan case. Reserve the liquid.
5 Blend the macerating liquid into the whipped cream to make the chantilly. Spread the chantilly over the strawberries, carefully smoothing the surface with a spatula.
6 Decorate the filled flan with whole strawberries and fresh mint leaves and serve.

● The flan case can be made 2–3 days ahead and kept in an airtight container. Once assembled, this flan has to be served immediately, otherwise the chantilly will soften the pastry and make it soggy.

Strawberry flan chantilly

Using Kitchen Equipment

MICROWAVE COOKING

The main advantage of the microwave oven is speed. It will defrost, heat or cook a wide variety of foods at a rate which an ordinary oven cannot match, making it a valuable time-saving part of your kitchen equipment.

A family-sized beef casserole will take about 14 minutes to reheat in a microwave oven, four portions of vegetables will take about 2 minutes and a meal for one on a plate will take between 2–3 minutes. With record speeds like this it's little wonder that microwave ovens are steadily increasing in popularity. They are also easy to work and particularly ideal to use in conjunction with a freezer, as you do not have to remember to take things out of the freezer well in advance. You can defrost food quickly and then go on to reheat or cook it.

Other advantages are that a microwave oven will save fuel as well as time and there are fewer of the smells associated with conventional oven cooking. It operates from an ordinary electric socket and takes up less space than an electric or gas cooker. However, it is important that adequate space be allowed for the air vents to operate — instructions are given for each individual model in its accompanying instruction manual. The outlet vents must not be covered. Models built into kitchen units will be given air vents in the same way as conventional ones.

A basic 600–700 watt domestic microwave oven is large enough to take a 5.4–6.3 kg / 12–14 lb turkey. The range of controls varies from the very basic Defrost and Cook settings with a timer, to the very elaborate with variable controls offering up to 12 power levels or cooking speeds, some with micro touch controls. All have a timer.

How it works
In a conventional oven the interior and the food container are all heated. The heat is gradually passed first to the outer layers of the food and then to the centre. In a microwave oven, however, the microwaves penetrate straight through the container into the food causing the water molecules contained in it to vibrate at a very high speed so creating friction and heat. As a result the food is heated quickly but the container and the interior of the oven (which contain no water molecules) remain cool. However, you will still need oven gloves because eventually the container will become heated by the food itself.

Cooking by microwave energy is what's known as a 'moist' form of cooking and as a result it does not crisp or brown food. For ways of overcoming this see the section Using a microwave.

Suitable containers
Do not use metal containers as these reflect and interfere with the microwaves. Most tableware is suitable but see that there are no metal or gold rims on any of the dishes. Containers that will not withstand the temperature of boiling water or cannot be used in a dishwasher should be used only for defrosting food in the microwave.

Covering
Cover the container only if required to do so in the recipe. Glass lids and cling film are suitable for covering food which needs to keep its moisture during cooking but when covering dishes with cling film it must either be pierced to prevent ballooning, or be pulled back at one corner to allow steam to escape. Also, remember to take care when removing the cover, as the steam could scald you. If it is not specified in a recipe that a dish is covered, then it is assumed that it is cooked without a lid.

Using a microwave
Cooking as opposed to reheating with a microwave oven is also quicker than by conventional means. For instance, a jacket potato can take just eight minutes. But if you have more than one item in the oven, the cooking time will increase: four medium-sized jacket potatoes will take around 15 minutes.

There is little loss of colour, moisture or flavour during cooking in a microwave oven although because there is no browning effect there will be no crisp skin on a roast chicken, for example. Some microwave ovens have a browning element included, or food can be browned in a special 'browning dish' inside the microwave oven before it is cooked. However, browning dishes do not crisp the food. Alternatively, you can use a grill on a conventional oven to colour the food, either before or after the cooking.

Use less seasoning than you would normally. Salt has a toughening effect so use it sparingly. When cooking vegetables, season and toss them with butter after cooking.

Provided it is given the correct cooking time, food reheated in a microwave oven will not burn or dry out — rice stays light and fluffy, roast meat will keep moist and baby foods and bottles can be warmed in seconds.

Whenever possible, use a microwave oven in conjunction with other kitchen equipment:
● Boil water in a kettle to speed the cooking of rice, pasta and dehydrated foods.
● Use a frying-pan on the ordinary cooker to seal and brown meat and vegetables.
● Crisp and colour food after microwave cooking in the grill of your cooker.
● Prove white bread dough in the microwave oven then, bake it conventionally.

Standing time
Microwaves only penetrate foods to a depth of about 2 inches, so foods that are denser and thicker need to be left for a short while after cooking to ensure that they are cooked right through. Let the food stand in the container it has been cooked in.

Defrosting food from the freezer
Commercial and home frozen foods can be defrosted quickly and safely in a microwave oven. This should be done in two stages. Allow a period of time (see the chart) in the oven on the defrost setting. Then leave it to stand to allow the temperature of the food to even out before you reheat or cook it. Only frozen vegetables can be cooked without the standing time, straight from the freezer. The method of defrosting is safe and quick, so there is no need to remove food from the freezer a long time in advance.

Using a microwave with a freezer
● Serve batch-baked sausages, soups, pies and casseroles piping hot and fresh tasting.
● Pancakes, vol-au-vents and fillings are useful freezer stocks.

What the microwave cannot do
Most microwave cookers cannot brown food or crisp it except sometimes when the food is

Microwave defrosting chart

Type of food	Amount	How many minutes in oven (approx)	How many minutes standing time (approx)
whole chicken	1.4 kg /3 lb	27	30–45
chicken portions	500 g /1 lb	10	10
joint of beef	1.4 kg /3 lb	26	40–60
stewing steak	500 g /1 lb	8	5
minced beef	500 g /1 lb	8	5
prawns	250 g /8 oz	4	5
trout	500 g /1 lb	9½	10
haddock fillets	500 g /1 lb	5	5
strawberries	500 g /1 lb	4	10
beef casserole	4 portions	24	10
chicken casserole	6 portions	40	15
white sauce	300 ml /10 fl oz	6½	5
thick soup	600 ml /1 pt	12	10
meal on a plate	350 g /12 oz	3½	2
sponge cake	family size	2	10
cheese cake	family size	2½	20
fruit crumble	family size	12	10
meat pie	family size	7	10
pancakes	6	2	2
croissants	6	1½	3
white loaf	large	6	10

in special containers. It is therefore not suitable for dishes like meringues, or Yorkshire pudding or roast vegetables. Eggs should never be cooked in their shells in a microwave oven as pressure builds up within the shell and they explode. Pulses are probably better cooked conventionally but they can be cooked in a microwave oven.

Adapting recipes

As a general rule all dishes that are boiled, steamed or baked can be adapted for the microwave oven. Dishes which require a crisp finish cannot be successfully cooked solely with a microwave.

Cream of chicken soup

🕯 23 minutes

Serves 4
225 g /8 oz cooked chicken, skinned and
  chopped
5 ml /1 tsp lemon juice
a pinch of salt
a pinch of white pepper
a pinch of ground nutmeg
75 ml /3 fl oz thick cream
50 g /2 oz butter
toasted almond slivers, to garnish
Microwave bechamel sauce
25 g /1 oz butter
25 g /1 oz flour
600 ml /1 pt chicken stock

1   To make the Microwave bechamel sauce, place the butter in a 1.4–1.7 L /2½–3 pt microwave casserole dish and melt it, covered, for 1 minute on High. Stir in the flour and continue cooking for a further 30 seconds on High.
2   In a separate microwave container, heat the stock for 2 minutes on High, then gradually mix it into the flour mixture. Return to the microwave oven for 8 minutes, stirring every 3 minutes with a whisk to blend it thoroughly.
3   Add the cooked chicken and lemon juice to the sauce and cook it for 5 minutes on High.
4   Pour the chicken sauce mixture into the goblet of an electric blender and process it to a purée.
5   Return the purée to the casserole dish, season it with salt, pepper and nutmeg and cook it for a further 4 minutes on High.
6   Place the cream in a small bowl and add some of the hot soup. Stir it well, then pour the mixture back into the soup. Cook for 2–3 minutes on High.
7   Cut the butter into small pieces, then stir it into the soup one piece at a time. Adjust the seasoning, transfer the soup to a tureen and sprinkle the almonds over the surface. Serve immediately.

Prawn-stuffed trout

🕯 20 minutes,
  including standing time

Serves 4
4 × 275 g /10 oz trout, cleaned
juice of 1 lemon
For the stuffing
50 g /2 oz butter
75 g /3 oz day-old white breadcrumbs
100 g /4 oz peeled prawns, chopped
grated zest of 1 lemon
1 medium-sized egg, beaten
salt and freshly ground black pepper

1   Make the stuffing. Put the butter in a mixing bowl and microwave it on High for 1½ minutes, until melted.
2   Remove it and stir in the breadcrumbs and prawns. Add the grated lemon zest and season with salt and pepper. Add the egg and mix well to combine the stuffing.
3   Divide the stuffing into 4 portions and stuff each trout. Place the trout on a serving dish and squeeze the lemon juice over them.
4   Microwave the trout, covered with cling film, on High for 12–15 minutes, or until the fish is cooked (when the skin comes away easily). Allow the trout to stand for 3 minutes before serving them.
5   For a crispy brown finish, after standing, place the fish under the hot grill for 2 minutes each side, then serve at once.

Sweet and sour beef

🕯 22 minutes

Serves 4–6
30 ml /2 tbls oil
2 large red peppers, cored, seeded and cut
  into thin strips
1 onion, peeled and finely chopped
1 large garlic clove, crushed
700 g /1½ lb rump steak, trimmed and
  cut into thin strips
For the sauce
30 ml /2 tbls cornflour
15 ml /1 tbls soy sauce
300 ml /½ pt beef stock
30 ml /2 tbls tomato purée
30 ml /2 tbls red wine vinegar
30 ml /2 tlbs clear honey

1   To make the sauce, place the cornflour in a bowl and blend in the soy sauce and beef stock, then mix in the tomato purée, vinegar and honey. Set it aside.
2   Place the oil, peppers, onion and garlic in a shallow microwave casserole dish. Cover it and cook for 3 minutes on High.
3   Add the meat to the casserole dish, cover it and cook it for a further 10 minutes on High, stirring once. Remove the meat from the casserole and keep it hot.
4   Add the sauce to the casserole dish and cook it for 6 minutes on High, stirring every two minutes.
5   Return the meat to the casserole dish and cook it for another 3 minutes on High. Stir it well, then serve immediately.

Carnival fish kebabs with Yellow rice

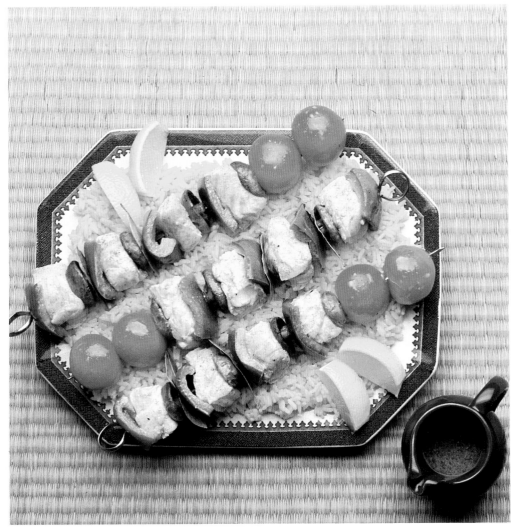

Chicken in red wine

This is a version of the French dish, *Coq au vin*. Using a microwave oven you can prepare and cook it in less than half the normal time.

🕐 37 minutes,
including standing time

Serves 4
1.8 kg /4 lb chicken
30 ml /2 tbls seasoned flour
25 g /1 oz butter
2 slices green back bacon, chopped
12 small onions
275 ml /10 fl oz red wine
275 ml /10 fl oz chicken stock
bouquet garni
salt and freshly ground black pepper

1   Skin and joint the chicken, and coat it in seasoned flour.
2   Put the butter in a microwave casserole dish and microwave on High for 1 minute. Add the chopped bacon and the whole onions to the butter and microwave them for 3 minutes.
3   Add all other ingredients. Season with salt and pepper. Cover the casserole dish with a lid or cling film and microwave on High for 15 minutes.
4   Stir the chicken and cook it for a further 8–10 minutes or until the chicken is done. To test, pierce it with a skewer: when the juices run clear the chicken is cooked. Then allow the chicken to stand for 10 minutes before serving.

Carnival fish kebabs

🕐 20 minutes,
plus 2 hours marinating

Serves 4
1 green pepper
16 button mushrooms, with stalks removed
450 g /1 lb cod fillets, skinned and cut into
   2.5 mm /1 in cubes
1 clove garlic, halved
8 bay leaves
8 small, firm tomatoes
For the marinade
45 ml /3 tbls olive oil
30 ml /2 tbls lemon juice
a pinch of salt
a pinch of black pepper
5 ml /1 tsp dried oregano
To serve
Yellow rice (see recipe)

1   Core and seed the pepper and cut it into 2.5 ml /1 in cubes. To blanch the cubes, put them into a small microwave bowl with 30 ml /2 tbls water and cook them for 2½ minutes on High. Let them stand for 5 minutes, then drain.
2   Meanwhile, prepare the marinade. Mix all the ingredients together in a large glass mixing bowl. Add the cod, green pepper and mushrooms and set them aside to marinate for 2 hours. Stir once or twice.
3   Rub 4 wooden kebab skewers with the

cut garlic clove for a light, subtle flavour.
4   Use a slotted spoon to remove the kebab ingredients from the marinade, reserving the marinade.
5   Arrange the cod, green pepper, mushrooms, bay leaves and tomatoes on the skewers. Put a microwave roasting rack in the oven and place the skewers onto the rack. Baste them with the reserved marinade.
6   Cook the kebabs for 10–13 minutes on High, or until the fish is cooked through and flakes easily when tested with a fork.
7   Transfer the skewers onto a hot serving dish and keep them warm. Place the remaining marinade and juices from the roasting rack into a small microwave bowl and heat for 1 minute on High. Pour over the kebabs and serve them at once with Yellow rice.

Yellow rice

🕐 34 minutes,
including standing time

Serves 4–6
15 g /½ oz butter
1 small onion, finely chopped
225 g /8 oz long-grain rice
a pinch of salt
2.5 ml /½ tsp ground turmeric
700 ml /1¼ pints boiling water

1   Place the butter and onion into a 1.7 L / 3 pint microwave casserole dish and cook uncovered for 2 minutes on High.
2   Add the rice, stir the mixture, cover and cook for a further 2 minutes on high.
3   Stir in the salt, turmeric and boiling water. Cover again and cook for a further 15–20 minutes on Medium or until all the water is absorbed and the rice is tender. Let it stand for 10 minutes before serving.

Tropical crumble

🕐 9–11 minutes

Serves 4–6
4 oranges, peeled with the white pith removed,
   and chopped
4 fresh apricots, stoned and chopped, or
   8 canned apricot halves, drained and chopped
2 large bananas, peeled and sliced
100 g /4 oz chopped fresh pineapple or canned
   pineapple chunks, drained
30 ml /2 tbls toasted dessicated coconut
For the topping
100 g /4 oz flour
2.5 ml /½ tsp ground ginger
25 g /1 oz rolled or porridge oats
25 g /1 oz dessicated coconut
150 g /5 oz light soft brown sugar
65 g /2½ oz butter
For decoration
dessicated coconut, toasted

1   Place all the fruit into a 1.4 L /2½ pt microwave casserole dish, turning the banana slices in the juices to prevent discoloration. Set it aside.
2   To make the topping, sift the flour and ginger into a large mixing bowl. Add the

oats, coconut and sugar and mix them together until they are well combined.
3   Place the butter in a small microwave bowl and cook it for 1 minute on High, then

stir it into the large bowl of dry ingredients.
4 Sprinkle the topping evenly over the fruit and press it down gently to level the surface.
5 Cook the mixture for 8–10 minutes on High or until the fruit mixture is just bubbling up around the edges of the topping. Serve the crumble, hot or chilled, with the toasted coconut sprinkled over the top.

Walnut chocolate cake

🕰 13–15 minutes, including standing time, plus cooling and finishing

Makes 6–8 portions
175 g /6 oz margarine, plus extra for greasing
175 g /6 oz soft light brown sugar
3 eggs
75 g /3 oz chopped walnuts
200 g /7 oz flour
25 g /1 oz cocoa
7.5 ml /1½ tsp baking powder
a pinch of salt
30 ml /2 tbls milk
Chocolate filling (page 105)

1 Line the base of a 20 cm /8 in soufflé dish with greaseproof paper. Grease the sides and base of the dish.
2 In a bowl, cream the margarine and sugar together until they are light and fluffy. Add the eggs, one at a time, beating well after each addition.
3 Fold in all the dry ingredients and then pour in the milk.
4 Pour the mixture into the soufflé dish and microwave on Medium for 8–10 minutes, or until the cake just comes away from the sides of the dish.
5 Allow the cake to stand for 5 minutes before turning it out onto a rack.
6 When the cake is cold, slice it horizontally into 3 layers and sandwich it together with Chocolate filling.

Mulled wine

🕰 45 minutes, including standing time

Makes about 20 glasses
850 ml /1½ pt water
4 lemons, juice reserved and rind finely chopped
2 oranges, juice reserved and rind finely chopped
125 g /4 oz sugar
2 × 3 in cinnamon sticks
2 × bottles red wine
150 ml /5 fl oz brandy
3 oranges, studded with about 50 cloves

1 Measure the water into a 4.5 L /8 pt microwave casserole dish. Add the lemon and orange juice to the casserole dish with the rinds, sugar and cinnamon sticks. Microwave the liquid on High for 15 minutes, stirring once or twice to dissolve the sugar. Leave the liquid to stand for 10 minutes.
2 Strain the liquid through a fine gauge sieve. Press the skins lightly with a wooden spoon to extract the juice, then discard them and the cinnamon sticks.
3 Pour the red wine into the casserole dish, add the prepared syrup, brandy and oranges with cloves.
4 Microwave for approximately 20 minutes on High. Do not allow it to boil. Ladle it into heatproof glasses or a large bowl and serve at once, re-heating as necessary.

Tropical crumble

FOOD PROCESSORS

Food processors prove invaluable when ingredients need to be puréed, blended, chopped or grated, as in the following appetizing recipes. They perform all these functions — and many more — efficiently and at speed.

A food processor consists of a strong motor encased in a housing onto which a bowl is fixed. The bowl is used with a selection of grating and slicing discs and blades. It is a compact appliance that is easy to use and simple to clean — in general the removable parts can be put in a dishwasher.

What will a food processor do?

A food processor has the ability to chop, mince, grind, slice and shred a variety of raw and cooked ingredients with speed. It does this, too, with the minimum of changing gadgets. This makes it particularly useful for preparing root vegetables for cooking, taking the time-consuming work out of shredding vegetables, grating cheese and chocolate, making breadcrumbs, zesting citrus peel and producing pâtés and stuffings from ingredients of differing densities.

A food processor will perform most of the functions of any other electric mixer, in terms of mixing, whisking and whipping. However, in most food processors the blade is either flat or just slightly curved at the ends, which means that it does not get as much air as another mixer into items such as egg whites and cake mixes. As a result, it is more efficient for making cakes by the all-in-one method or from packet mixes. For a good volume of egg white, you will need a hand-held electric mixer (unless you have a model with a special whisk attachment).

For puréeing or blending, most food processors hold a smaller volume than a blender. Therefore large quantities of soup or fruit purée have to be processed in batches. However, processors do not require liquid when blending, so it is often possible to blend just the solid matter, then combine the purée and liquid later.

Which machine to buy?

Machines vary in capacity, controls, ease of use and attachments available.

For most families, a standard-size bowl is sufficient. Models with very small bowls are only suitable for a kitchen with one or two people, otherwise you lose the advantage of speed by having to process several batches in sequence. A very large food processor is a real boon to anyone who prepares food in large quantities, but can be rather less useful when slicing just a couple of onions or making one-egg mayonnaise.

Controls are either an on/off switch or a turn of the lid in its fixed position to operate the motor. Some models have a pulse button which gives an on/off motion. This is useful for processing foods which you want to blend with other ingredients without cutting them too much — for example dried fruit into an all-in-one cake mixture. This is also useful for cutting evenly sized pieces of solid food such as meat.

The advantage of switches is that they leave your hands free to feed food into the bowl. Their disadvantage is that it is easier to overprocess. Lid-operated machines obviate this risk to some extent and cannot be switched on accidentally, making them safer in homes where there are small children. It is possible to simulate the pulse action by moving the lid backwards and forwards rapidly.

Its variety of attachments gives a food processor its versatility. Most models come with a chopping (knife) blade, a slicing disc and a shredding disc. Other attachments may include a chipper disc, whisk, pulping disc and plastic blade for making dough.

Food processor tips:

● Keep the food processor permanently on a work surface so that a special effort is not necessary for using it.
● Never immerse it in water.
● Store the bowl, the cutters and the lid on the motor housing. If the lid has a feed tube, leave the presser out during storing so that the bowl is well ventilated.
● Practise until you discover the time needed to chop or mince; it is only too easy to reduce foods to a purée!
● For slicing, shredding and grating, chill the foods first.
● For small quantities of icing, sauce or mayonnaise, use a folded tea-towel under one corner of the machine, so that the bowl is slightly tilted and the blade can get right into the mixture.

Liver and hazelnut pâté

 1 hour 20 minutes,
 plus soaking and standing

Serves 6

500 g /1 lb pig's liver, sliced
milk, for soaking
1 medium-sized onion
250 g /8 oz streaky bacon, rinded
oil, for frying and greasing
10 juniper berries
50 g /2 oz brown breadcrumbs
50 g /2 oz hazelnuts, shelled
salt
freshly ground black pepper

1 Put the pig's liver in a bowl and cover it with milk. Leave to soak for an hour before cooking (to tone down its strong flavour). Chop the onion coarsely in the food processor.
2 Heat the oven to 180C /350F /gas 4. Fry the bacon and onion in a little oil for 5 minutes. Add the pig's liver and juniper berries and fry for 10 minutes, turning the mixture frequently.

3 Allow the contents of the pan to cool and, using the knife blade, work in the food processor until a coarse purée is formed.
4 Add the breadcrumbs, hazelnuts and seasoning to the processor and blend for a further 15 seconds.
5 Place the pâté in an oiled 750 g /1½ lb loaf tin and cover with foil. Stand the tin in a roasting pan and pour in boiling water to come halfway up the tin. Place in the oven for 1 hour.
6 Remove the pâté from the oven. Place weights on the top and leave it for several hours, preferably overnight. Turn out and serve it cut in thick slices.

Provençal tartlets

These tartlets are ideal for a drinks party. Do not freeze them for more than a month, or the flavours will become too strong.

 1 hour,
 plus cooling

Makes about 50

butter, for greasing
black olive slices, for decorating
For the pastry
250 g /8 oz flour
salt
cayenne pepper
a pinch of mustard powder
100 g /4 oz butter, diced
100 g /4 oz Cheddar cheese, grated
1 egg yolk
For the filling
450 g /1 lb tomatoes, blanched, skinned and
  chopped
90 ml /6 tbls olive oil
1 garlic clove, crushed
3 fresh basil leaves or a pinch of dried basil
freshly ground black pepper
50 g /2 oz canned anchovy fillets
125 g /4½ oz soft cream cheese
50 g /2 oz black olives, stoned and sliced

1 Heat the oven to 200C /400F /gas 6. Grease fifty 5 cm /2 in tart tins.
2 Place the flour, salt, cayenne pepper and mustard in the food processor on the knife blade. Add the diced butter and blend until the mixture resembles fine crumbs.
3 Add the cheese and blend until well mixed. Add the egg yolk and 15 ml /1 tbls water and blend until the pastry forms a ball and comes away from the sides of the bowl.
4 Remove the dough from the bowl and chill while you prepare the filling.
5 To make the filling, cook the tomatoes in the oil until soft. Place them in the food processor bowl on the knife blade together with all the other ingredients, including the oil from the anchovies. Blend until a smooth cream is formed.
6 Roll the pastry out 3 mm /⅛ in thick. Using a 6 cm /2½ in pastry cutter, cut out 50 rounds and fit in the greased tart tins.
7 Place 15 ml /1 tbls filling in each tartlet shell and bake for 12–15 minutes. Cool and decorate each with some sliced black olive. Serve them warm or cold.

Buttered cauliflower towers

Buttered cauliflower towers

 1½–1¾ hours

Serves 6
1 large cauliflower, about 1 kg /2 lb
150 ml /5 fl oz milk
salt
100 g /4 oz potato
3 eggs
50 g /2 oz softened butter
butter, for greasing
freshly ground black pepper
freshly grated nutmeg
To garnish
15–30 ml /1–2 tbls melted butter
15–30 ml /1–2 tbls finely chopped fresh parsley
sprigs of parsley
tiny wedges of lemon

1 Heat the oven to 190C /375F /gas 5. Trim the cauliflower into florets and rinse them in cold water.
2 In a large pan, bring the milk and 1.1 L /2 pt salted water to the boil. Cook the florets in this liquid for 10–15 minutes, or until they are just tender. Drain well.
3 Meanwhile, peel and quarter the potato, cook in boiling salted water for 15–20 minutes. Drain thoroughly and mash the potato.
4 Purée the cooked florets in the food processor. Beat in the mashed potato, eggs and softened butter. Season with salt, freshly ground black pepper and nutmeg.
5 Line the base of 6 dariole moulds (150 ml /5 fl oz capacity) with greaseproof paper. Butter the base and sides of the moulds and fill them with the cauliflower mixture. Cover the moulds with buttered foil.
6 Place the filled moulds in a pan or gratin dish containing 25 mm /1 in simmering water, and bake them in the oven for 35–40 minutes.
7 Remove the dish from the oven and leave it to stand for a few minutes. Unmould the cauliflower towers onto a warm serving dish. (Often it is easier to unmould the towers onto an individual plate and transfer them to a serving dish with a fish slice.)
8 To garnish, brush with melted butter and sprinkle with finely chopped parsley, then arrange the parsley sprigs and tiny lemon wedges around the base of the towers.

Sunset salad

 10 minutes

Serves 6
1 medium-sized onion
450 g /1 lb red cabbage
2 carrots
2 red peppers, seeded
25 g /1 oz dates, stoned
For the dressing
30 ml /2 tbls olive oil
5 ml /1 tsp French mustard
5 ml /1 tsp sugar
salt and freshly ground black pepper
15 ml /1 tbls red wine vinegar

1 With the knife blade in position in the food processor bowl, chop the onion coarsely.
2 Remove the onion and the blade and put the grating disc in position. Grate the cabbage and carrots into the bowl. Replace the grating disc with the slicing disc and push the red peppers and dates through.
3 Stir all the ingredients for the dressing together, then add it to the salad before serving.

Pineapple and orange soufflé

Pineapple and orange soufflé

🍴 1 hour,
plus cooling and chilling

Serves 6

1 medium-sized pineapple, peeled and cored
60 ml /4 tbls fresh orange juice
25 ml /1½ tbls gelatine
4 medium-sized eggs, separated
75 g /3 oz caster sugar
30 ml /2 tbls kirsch
150 ml /5 fl oz yoghurt
150 ml /5 fl oz thick cream
ratafia biscuits and thin strips of orange zest,
to decorate

1 Tie a paper collar onto an 850 ml /1½ pt soufflé dish.
2 Cut the pineapple in the food processor on the knife blade. Blend until it forms a not-too-smooth purée.
3 Place the orange juice in a cup in a pan of warm water and sprinkle the gelatine over the orange. Leave it to dissolve.
4 Put the egg yolks, caster sugar and kirsch in a heatproof bowl and stand it in a pan of hot water over a gentle heat. Whisk continuously until the mixture becomes pale and thickens.
5 Remove the bowl from the pan and stir in the pineapple purée. Take a large spoonful of the mixture and stir it into the cup of gelatine liquid. Pour this back into the pineapple mixture and whisk in well.
6 Leave to cool, but not set, whisking from time to time. When the mixture is cool, whip the yoghurt and cream together until thick and fold it into the pineapple mixture. Beat the egg whites until they are stiff and fold the pineapple mixture into them.

7 Pour into the prepared soufflé dish and chill for several hours. To serve, remove the paper collar and decorate the sides and top of the soufflé with ratafias and orange zest.

English fig tart

🍴 making the pastry case,
then 1½ hours, including chilling

Serves 6–8

250 g /8 oz plain flour
5 ml /1 tsp icing sugar
2.5 ml /½ tsp salt
150 g /5 oz cold butter,
plus extra for greasing
1 egg yolk
5 ml /1 tsp lemon juice
30 ml /2 tbls iced water
1 egg white, beaten
800 g /1¾ lb canned figs
30 ml /2 tbls icing sugar
15 ml /1 tbls kirsch
150 ml /5 fl oz thick cream
For the almond filling
2 eggs
75 ml /5 tbls caster sugar
100 g /4 oz ground almonds
90 ml /6 tbls thick cream
juice and finely grated zest of 1 large lemon
1–2 drops almond essence

1 Place the flour, icing sugar and salt in the food processor on the knife blade. Add the butter and blend until the mixture resembles crumbs.
2 Add the egg yolk, lemon juice and water and blend until the pastry forms a ball and comes away from the sides of the bowl.
3 Remove the dough and chill it in the refrigerator for at least one hour.
4 Grease a 23 cm /9 in baking tin. Roll out the pastry to 3 mm /⅛ in thick and press it into the tin from the base outwards. Prick the base with a fork and chill for ½ hour.

5 Heat the oven to 200C /400F /gas 6.
6 Line the pastry with foil and beans and bake for 10 minutes. Turn the oven down to 180C /350F /gas 4 and bake the case for a further 8–10 minutes without the foil. Allow it to cool.
7 Brush the half-baked pastry shell with the beaten egg white. Leave the prepared pastry case in its tin on a baking sheet. Heat the oven to 200C /400F /gas 6.
8 Prepare the almond filling; in the food processor whisk the eggs with the caster sugar until thick and creamy. Add the ground almonds, thick cream, juice and finely grated zest of lemon and the almond essence. Beat until blended.
9 Fill the pastry case with the almond mixture and bake for 30 minutes until it is puffed and firm to the touch. Remove the tart from the oven and cool.
10 Drain the figs and reserve the syrup. Cut the figs in half and drain on absorbent paper. Arrange the halves over the tart, leaving a narrow border around the edge.
11 Combine 50 ml /2 fl oz of the reserved fig syrup and the icing sugar and beat until the sugar has dissolved. Place in a pan over a medium heat and boil until the syrup has reduced to half the quantity. Add the kirsch and coat the figs with the syrup. Allow to cool, then chill.
12 Just before serving, whisk the cream until thick. Fill a piping bag fitted with a star nozzle and pipe round the edge of the tart.

Cherry cheesecake

🍴 1½ hours

Serves 6–8

150 g /5 oz digestive biscuits
25 g /1 oz ground almonds
75 g /3 oz butter, melted
For the filling
175 g /6 oz full-fat soft cheese
7.5 ml /1½ tsp clear honey
425 g /15 oz canned cherries
10 ml /2 tsp cornflour
30 ml /2 tbls redcurrant jelly
15 ml /1 tbls lemon juice
flaked almonds, to decorate

1 Process the biscuits and almonds until the mixture resembles fine crumbs. Add the butter and mix.
2 Press the mixture over the bottom and sides of a 20 cm /8 in shallow cake tin. Cover and chill for 30 minutes.
3 To make the filling: process the cheese and honey until smooth, then spread the mixture over the base.
3 Drain the cherries, reserving 125 ml /4 fl oz of syrup. Halve and stone the cherries and arrange them on the filling.
5 In a saucepan, blend the cornflour and cherry syrup to a smooth paste. Add the redcurrant jelly and lemon juice. Mix well.
6 Bring to the boil, stirring continuously, then simmer for 1–2 minutes until thick.
7 Spoon the glaze over the cherries. Chill until set. Sprinkle the top with almonds.

English fig tart

PRESSURE COOKING

A pressure cooker is a valuable aid because it cuts cooking time when you are most rushed. Time-consuming recipes become easier and quicker. A pressure cooker may seem daunting at first, but it is simple to use.

In an ordinary saucepan steam escapes from the top or around the lid and heat is lost, so that 100C /212F, or boiling temperature, is the highest temperature reached. With a pressure cooker there is a gasket inside the edge of the lid which produces an airtight seal when the lid is clamped into position. As you heat the pan and its contents, pressure builds up inside, so that the liquid reaches a much higher temperature. This higher temperature means that your food can be cooked in approximately one-third of the time which would be taken by using more conventional cooking methods.

Choosing a pressure cooker

Pressure cookers come in different sizes and you should go for the largest you can afford and store comfortably. Remember that you can only use one-third of the capacity given, as the cooker has to be two-thirds empty during cooking.

On the other hand, size is not a problem when cooking small quantities: the minimum amount of liquid necessary for a pressure cooker to work is 300 ml /10 fl oz so, unlike a saucepan, a pressure cooker cannot be too large. With normal use, a pressure cooker will last for many years.

Most pressure cookers are made of aluminium, which is a good material for spreading heat evenly. Some have a non-stick lining and you must decide if this is worth paying for: there is less likelihood of the food sticking if you fry or sauté it before pressure cooking, but remember that non-stick linings tend to scratch easily and need to be treated with care. Some models have enamelled exteriors in a choice of colours.

Pressure cookers usually come with some interior fittings. There is normally a trivet on which to stand food which is not directly cooked in liquid, such as Stuffed peppers (see recipe). Many pressure cookers also have a set of baskets for cooking different foods simultaneously, for example meat and vegetables. Others have a blanching basket or a solid unperforated basket for cooking delicate foods like stewed fruit or custards. Models that offer a choice of fittings — and pressures — are the most versatile.

Safety

Whatever model you buy, it is essential to read and understand the manufacturer's instructions. At one time pressure cookers had a name for being rather alarming devices which sometimes blew up. Fortunately modern models are equipped with safety plugs — if anything goes wrong, the plug blows and the steam escapes harmlessly, rather than blowing off the lid. Check your pressure cooker each time you use it to see that the valve or weights are not clogged up and that the rubber gasket has not perished. Should you need any spare parts, they are generally available from the stores that sell the pressure cookers.

Achieving the correct pressure

Pressure cookers can operate at different pressures and most have a choice of three — usually quoted as high, medium and low or 15, 10 and 5 lb. High pressure is used for cooking meat, vegetables and casseroles. Medium pressure is used for softening fruit for jams and jellies. Low pressure is for bottling fruit, for food containing raising agents and for more delicate dishes.

In some models, there is a visual pressure indicator incorporating a plunger which rises and falls with the pressure. In other models, you can tell when pressure is reached by the noise it makes. Cookers with only one pressure have a fixed pressure valve; when pressure is reached a valve on the lid rotates, then you lower the heat.

Reducing pressure: there are two ways of reducing pressure after cooking. One is to stand the cooker in a bowl of cold water or place it in an empty sink and run cold water on the lid, taking care not to allow any water to drip through the safety plug. This is the quickest method and is suitable for most ordinary cooking.

However, for foods which spoil with a sudden drop in temperature — like steamed puddings which would sink — remove the cooker from the heat and leave it until all the steam has gently evaporated.

Some expensive and sophisticated models depressurize automatically and quickly once removed from the heat.

Using your pressure cooker

Do remember that pressure cooking requires very accurate timing. Because it is so fast, some foods can easily be reduced to a purée. Study your manufacturer's instructions carefully and follow the cooking times given there or in recipes. The liquid used must be one that produces steam; fat and oil alone are not sufficient. Do not overfill the cooker.

Remember, too, that since it is a form of closed cooking, dishes which might otherwise brown or turn golden when cooked conventionally will not take on colour. Plan to pre-fry the meat or finish the dish under the grill if necessary.

Beef tends to lose colour unless it is cooked with other ingredients which help it to retain its colour. On the other hand, red kidney beans will colour any food they are cooked with.

Correct seasoning is vital for pressure cooked food, since cooking is done too quickly for flavours to mingle. With dishes like curry you need to be sure you have got the balance of flavours right (see my recipe for Pork curry). For less highly seasoned dishes, it is best to under-season, adding more when cooking has been completed.

Supper soup

A pressure cooker makes short work of a long stewing job. Served with hunks of French bread, this dish is very filling and need only be followed by a green salad.

🔪 30 minutes

Serves 4
750 g /1½ lb scrag end of lamb
2 carrots, diced
2 celery sticks, chopped into 10 mm /½ in pieces
2 medium-sized potatoes, diced
1 medium-sized onion, sliced into thick rings
50 g /2 oz pearl barley
1 L /1¾ pt stock, home-made or from a cube
salt and freshly ground black pepper

1 Put all the ingredients into the pressure cooker and pressure cook on high for 20 minutes.
2 Let down the pressure under a cold running tap. Open the cooker and remove the meat from the pan.
3 Cut up the meat into small chunks, removing the bones, and return it to the pan. Serve steaming hot.

Stuffed peppers

20 minutes

Serves 4
4 medium-sized green peppers
25 g /1 oz cooked long-grain rice (15 g /½ oz raw weight)
1 medium-sized onion, finely chopped
200 g / 7 oz canned tuna, drained and flaked
½ red pepper, finely chopped
15 ml /1 tbls finely chopped fresh parsley
salt and freshly ground black pepper
50 g /2 oz cheese, grated

1 Cut off the tops of the peppers and remove the membranes and seeds, taking care not to perforate the base. Check that each pepper will stand on its base and trim a little off the bottom if necessary.
2 Mix the cooked rice with the onion, tuna, pepper and parsley. Season well and place the mixture inside the peppers.
3 Put 300 ml /10 fl oz water in the cooker; stand the peppers on the trivet. Pressure cook at high for 4 minutes. Heat the grill.
4 Let down the pressure under a cold running tap. Top each pepper with grated cheese and grill briefly until golden.

Braised rump

1¼ hours

Serves 6
30 ml /2 tbls vegetable oil
1 kg /2 lb top rump, in one piece
2 medium-sized onions, sliced
2 celery sticks, chopped
6 medium-sized carrots, sliced
4 medium-sized potatoes, sliced
1 pig's trotter
300 ml /10 fl oz cider
300 ml /10 fl oz stock, home-made or from a cube
5 ml /1 tsp dried mixed herbs
salt and freshly ground black pepper

1 Heat the oil in the pressure cooker. Fry the rump until browned, then remove it.
2 Mix the prepared vegetables and place them in the base of the cooker.
3 Place the joint of meat on top, tuck the pig's trotter down the side and add the liquids and seasonings.
4 Pressure cook at medium for 1 hour, then release the pressure under a cold running tap. Remove the trotter. The braised rump is equally good served hot or cold.

Pork curry

30 minutes

Serves 4
500 g /1 lb lean boneless pork, cut into cubes
50 g /2 oz seasoned flour
30 ml /2 tbls vegetable oil
2 medium-sized onions, chopped
2 garlic cloves, crushed
5 ml /1 tsp ground coriander
5 ml /1 tsp ground cumin
5 ml /1 tsp chilli powder
2 celery sticks, cut into 10 mm /½ in pieces
2 carrots, diced
½ red pepper, cut into strips
5 ml /1 tsp wine vinegar
15 ml /1 tbls sweet chutney
15 ml /1 tbls tomato purée
25 g /1 oz sultanas
300 ml /10 fl oz stock, home-made or from a cube
salt and freshly ground black pepper

1 Toss the meat in the seasoned flour.
2 Heat the oil in the pressure cooker and gently fry the onion.
3 Add the meat and fry until the cubes are brown on all sides. Add the garlic and spices, and continue to cook gently for about 3 minutes, stirring all the time. Add the remaining ingredients and mix well.
4 Pressure cook for 20 minutes on high. Release the pressure under a cold running tap and serve immediately.

Paprika beanpot

45 minutes

Serves 4
225 g /8 oz cannellini or haricot beans
500 g /1 lb onions, sliced into rings
2 garlic cloves, chopped
1 green pepper, seeded and cut into strips
1 red pepper, seeded and cut into strips
30 ml /2 tbls vegetable oil
400 g /14 oz canned tomatoes
90 ml /6 tbls tomato purée
15 ml /1 tbls paprika
5 ml /1 tsp sugar
salt and freshly ground black pepper
150 ml /5 fl oz soured cream
finely chopped fresh parsley, to garnish

1 Soak the beans in hot water to cover for 15–30 minutes. During this time, prepare the other vegetables.
2 Heat the oil in the base of the pressure cooker. Gently fry the onions and garlic for a few minutes, then add the other ingredients except for the soured cream and parsley. Drain the beans and add them.
3 Pressure cook on high for 15 minutes. Release the pressure under a cold running tap.
4 Remove the lid and return the pan to the hob uncovered. Boil gently to reduce any surplus liquid. Stir in the soured cream and parsley and serve.

Stuffed peppers

MAKING THE MOST OF YOUR FREEZER

Cooking for, and from, the freezer is a great time-saver. My basic meat mixtures can be made into several tasty main course dishes, then frozen; my lovely summer fruit desserts can be enjoyed long after the season is over.

Every cook, from time to time, has been required to produce a meal without being able to get to the shops. This is when the freezer comes into its own. In this section I give you some excellent recipes for freezing, and tips on how best to use your freezer.

Freezing meat

Cooking meat from frozen can be a real life-saver when you have to produce a meal in a hurry. Most cuts will cook from frozen successfully. On-the-bone joints weighing up to 2.7 kg /6 lb and stewing steak can also be cooked without thawing first.

There are, however, some meats which must be thawed thoroughly before cooking — otherwise they are unsafe. Whole chicken should always be thawed first because there is always a risk that bacteria in the meat will not be destroyed if a sufficiently high temperature had not been reached.

Rolled joints like breast of lamb or boned and rolled loin must be thawed before cooking too. This is because the meat has been handled during rolling and thorough cooking is necessary to destroy bacteria.

It is also best to thaw joints for pot-roasting and boiling, as well as roasting joints over 2.7 /kg 6 lb, as it is difficult to prevent the outside overcooking before the inside is done.

Freezing cuts and sausages

To get the best results when cooking from frozen, it is worth taking extra care when either preparing meat for the freezer or buying it frozen. Never refreeze previously thawed raw meat.

The following types of meat are excellent choices for family meals. Remember to use proper thick freezer polythene bags to exclude as much air as possible when packing the items.

Steaks: when freezing steaks, make sure each one is quite flat. If it is curled or doubled over it will need to be thawed to ensure even contact with the pan. Either wrap each steak in a strong polythene bag or

interleave a number with freezer paper. Keep them on a flat level surface until frozen.

Chops: open freeze chops — spread them out in a single layer on a baking tray until they are hard, then pack them in a polythene bag. Alternatively, interleave with freezer paper and overwrap with foil, packing in fours or sixes, whichever is most convenient.

Sausages: buy the individually frozen ones or open freeze your own so you can take out the number you need, rather than having to prise a block apart or wait for it to thaw.

Stewing meat: you can buy free-flow frozen packs of cubed casseroling meat, but if your butcher is cutting it for you, open freeze the pieces before packing them in strong polythene bags. The small individual pieces will quickly thaw over a gentle heat. You will then have to use a pressure cooker if you are in a hurry to get the meat tender.

Cooking frozen cuts and sausages

To grill frozen steaks or chops, brush the meat with oil, and place it about 5 cm /2 in further away from the heat than usual. When the meat is almost cooked, move it nearer to the heat and continue cooking until it is brown. Now turn and brown the other side.

To fry frozen steaks, chops, or sausages put a little fat in the pan and start cooking at a lower than usual temperature. When cooking is almost complete, raise the temperature to brown the meat. Turn once during cooking.

Timing for both grilling and frying will depend on the thickness of the meat and how well you like it cooked, but expect it to take 5–10 minutes longer than when cooking from thawed.

To cook frozen stewing meat, put the cubes of meat into a casserole, together with the vegetables and liquids, and cook for 30 minutes longer than usual.

Cooking frozen joints

To cook a frozen joint successfully, you will need a meat thermometer. But first you will need to calculate the cooking time according

to how well done you like your meat. The chart below gives the cooking times and the internal cooked temperature necessary.

Roast the meat at 180C /350F /gas 4 and, about 20 minutes before the end of the calculated time, plunge the meat thermometer into the centre of the meat. If the meat is on the bone you must position the thermometer as near to the bone as possible without actually touching it. Cook until the correct internal temperature is reached.

With some models of thermometer you are instructed to insert the thermometer before cooking. This is obviously impossible if the meat is frozen solid — in which case insert the thermometer as soon as the meat has thawed enough.

Freezing fruit

The way you freeze summer fruit depends on the type of fruit and how you are likely to use it once it has thawed. Select the appropriate method from the following list. Summer fruit treated in any of these ways can be frozen for up to a year.

Dry pack

This means freezing fruit without sugar. It is the best method for tough-skinned fruit like blackcurrants and gooseberries. They will not

Roasting frozen joints: at 180C /350F /gas 4

Weight	Cooking	Minutes per kg	Minutes per lb	Thermometer
Beef: under	well done	75 + 35 extra	35 + 35 extra	79C /170F
1.8 kg /4 lb	medium rare	65 + 30 extra	30 + 30 extra	71C /160F
Beef: 1.8–2.7 kg /	well done	90 + 40 extra	40 + 40 extra	79C /170F
4–6 lb	medium/rare	75 + 35 extra	35 + 35 extra	71C /160F
Lamb: under	well done	75 + 35 extra	35 + 35 extra	82C /180F
1.8 kg /4 lb	pinkish	65 + 30 extra	30 + 30 extra	71C /160F
Lamb: 1.8–2.7 kg /	well done	90 + 40 extra	40 + 40 extra	82C /180F
4–6 lb	pinkish	75 + 35 extra	35 + 35 extra	71C /160F
Pork: under	well done	75 + 35 extra	35 + 35 extra	88C /190F
1.8 kg /4 lb				
Pork: 1.8–2.7 kg /	well done	100 + 45 extra	45 + 45 extra	88C /190F
4–6 lb				

stick together when frozen. Wash the fruit only if absolutely necessary and then blot it dry. To prepare the fruit you simply fork currants off their stems, or top and tail gooseberries, or divide rhubarb into short lengths. Next, put the prepared fruit into polythene bags, seal, label and freeze.

This is also a quick and easy way to deal with fruit such as hulled raspberries and blackberries if you are in a hurry.

Use dry packed fruit when thawed in the same way as fresh. Add them almost, but not completely, thawed to fruit salads or use them to make jams or chutneys.

Open freezing
The fruit suitable for dry packing can also be open frozen. To open freeze berries, spread them out in a single layer on a baking tray until they are frozen hard, then pack them into polythene bags. Frozen in this way, each fruit remains separate, so you can just tip out the quantity you need, when you need it, and return the rest to the freezer. Use in the same ways as dry packed frozen fruits.

Sugar pack
By this method sugar is added to the fruit before freezing. It is a good way to freeze soft fruit like raspberries and blackberries which make their own juice. Allow about 125 g /4 oz sugar to 500 g /1 lb fruit. Prepare the fruit and either mix it gently with the sugar and then spoon it straight into strong polythene bags, or layer fruit and sugar into rigid containers. Next, seal, label and freeze. When the fruit are thawed they will be swimming in their own sweetened juices. Use in summer puddings or serve with cream or ice cream.

Sugar syrup
Firm fruit like apricots, peaches, greengages, plums and cherries are best frozen in syrup. The proportion of sugar to water depends on the tartness of the fruit and your own taste. A light syrup using 200 g /8 oz sugar to 500 ml /1 pt water is a good all-purpose strength, though damsons and tart plums may need a medium strength syrup — 250 g /10 oz sugar to 500 ml /1 pt water.

Use syrup pack fruit in pies and crumbles, with sponge puddings and to serve in compotes. Apple rings frozen in syrup can be used for decorating too.

Purées
Any damaged or over-ripe fruit can be turned into a purée. Hard fruit will need cooking with a little water and 125–200 g /4–6 oz sugar per 500 g /1 lb fruit before sieving. Soft fruit only need sieving and can be sweetened or not as you please; 500 g /1 lb of fruit will produce about 300 ml /10 fl oz purée. Pack the purée in 300 ml /10 fl oz containers, leaving 10 mm /½ in headspace. Seal, label and freeze. Use purées for fools (see Gooseberry fool), mousses, ice creams and sauces.

Basic beef mixture

 3 hours

Makes 3 casseroles
3.5 kg /7 lb braising steak
175 g /6 oz flour, well seasoned with salt and freshly ground black pepper
175 ml /6 fl oz oil, for frying
500 g /1 lb onions, sliced
1 L /1¾ pt red wine
1 stock cube

1 Heat the oven to 180C /350F /gas 4. Trim the meat and cut it into 25 mm /1 in cubes. Put the seasoned flour in a plastic bag and shake the meat cubes in the bag until they are thoroughly coated with flour. Next, shake off any excess.
2 Divide the oil between a large frying-pan and a large flameproof casserole. Add the onions to the frying-pan and fry until soft and translucent. Remove to a large mixing bowl using a slotted spoon.
3 Fry the meat in batches simultaneously in the frying-pan and casserole over a medium-high heat until each piece is browned all over. Add each batch to the mixing bowl using a slotted spoon. When all the meat is browned transfer it and the onions to the casserole.
4 Add the wine and stock cube and cover. Cook in the oven for 2 hours or until the meat is tender.
5 Remove the casserole from the oven but do not switch off the heat if using the beef mixture straight away. Divide the mixture among 3 small casseroles, then proceed with the following recipes.

Red beef casserole

35 minutes before freezing, then 1 hour

Serves 4–6
450 g /1 lb beetroot, cooked
2 garlic cloves
⅓ of basic beef mixture
5 ml /1 tsp ground ginger

1 Heat the oven to 180C /350F /gas 4.
2 Roughly chop the beetroot, then blend it in an electric blender until it turns into a purée. You may need to add a little water if the beetroot has not been very well cooked, to soften the purée.
3 Crush the garlic and add it to the basic beef mixture in the casserole, together with the puréed beetroot and the ground ginger. Stir the mixture well and cover the casserole with a lid. Cook it in the oven for a further 20 minutes.
4 Take the casserole from the oven and allow it to cool. Next, transfer it to a freezer-proof container, seal, label and freeze for up to 6 months.

● To serve: thaw overnight in the refrigerator. Reheat at 180C /350F /gas 4 for 1 hour.

Hazelnut, beef and tomato casserole

71

Hazelnut, beef and tomato casserole

🍴 30 minutes before freezing, then 1 hour

Serves 4-6
400 g /14 oz canned tomatoes
30 ml /2 tbls tomato purée
50 g /2 oz hazelnuts, chopped
⅓ of basic beef mixture

1 Heat the oven to 180C /350F /gas 4.
2 Add the tomatoes, tomato purée and hazelnuts to the basic beef mixture.
3 Cover the casserole and cook in the oven for 20 minutes.
4 Take the casserole from the oven. Allow it to cool, then transfer it to a freezer-proof container. Seal it, then label and freeze for up to 6 months.

● To serve: thaw overnight in the refrigerator. Reheat at 180C /350F /gas 4 for 1 hour.

Orange, beef and celery casserole

🍴 40 minutes before freezing, then 1 hour

Serves 4-6
1 medium-sized orange
4 celery sticks, trimmed and chopped into 25 mm /1 in pieces
4 medium-sized carrots, pared and sliced thickly
⅓ of basic beef mixture

1 Heat the oven to 180C /350F /gas 4.
2 Thinly pare the zest from the orange and then cut it into short pieces using a sharp knife. Squeeze the juice from the orange.
3 Add the orange zest and juice, celery pieces and sliced carrots to the basic beef mixture in the casserole. Stir well and cover.
4 Cook the casserole in the oven for 20 minutes.
5 Take the casserole from the oven and let it cool. Now seal it in a freezer-proof container. Label the casserole and freeze it for up to 6 months.

● To serve: thaw overnight in the refrigerator. Reheat at 180C /350F /gas 4 for 1 hour.

Basic pork fillet preparation

This basic quantity makes 4 dishes: 4 of the pork fillets are fried, for making into 2 casseroles (see Paprika pork and Normandy pork); the other 4 fillets are kept whole for rolling (see Pork with port and Pork with prunes). As the rolls are frozen raw, do not use previously frozen meat.

🍴🍴 40 minutes

Gooseberry fool

Makes 4 dishes
8 fresh pork fillets, each weighing 400 g /14 oz
175 g /6 oz flour
15 ml /1 tbls salt
freshly ground black pepper
10 ml /2 tsp dried mixed herbs
90 ml /6 tbls oil, for frying
3 small onions, skinned and chopped

1 Select 4 of the most evenly-sized fillets. Trim off any loose bits of fat or flesh and reserve the trimmed fillets in the refrigerator for use in the recipes Pork with port and Pork with prunes.
2 Cut the other 4 fillets into 25 mm /1 in cubes. Put the flour, the salt, the pepper and the herbs into a polythene bag. Add the meat pieces, a few at a time, shake until well coated and discard any excess flour.
3 Using 2 large frying-pans, fry the cubes in the oil over a medium-high heat.
4 Divide the cooked meat between 2 casseroles and pour the meat juices into 1 frying-pan. Fry the onions in this pan, then transfer them to 1 of the casseroles for Paprika pork.

Paprika pork

🍴 1¼ hours before freezing, then 1 hour

Serves 4-6
½ the fried pork cubes with onion
15 ml /1 tbls oil
25 g /1 oz flour
30 ml /2 tbls paprika
600 ml /1 pt stock, home-made or from a cube
120 ml /8 tbls tomato purée
salt and freshly ground black pepper
To finish
250 g /8 oz button mushrooms, sliced
150 ml /5 fl oz soured cream
chopped fresh parsley, to garnish

1 Heat the oven to 190C /375F /gas 5. Put the pork cubes and onion into a casserole (if you have not done so already). Drain the juices into a frying-pan, add the oil and place over a moderate heat.
2 Stir in the flour and cook for 1 minute. Add the paprika and cook for a further minute. Take the pan from the heat and stir in the stock and the tomato purée. Season to taste with salt and pepper.
3 Bring to the boil, then pour the sauce over the meat in the casserole.
4 Cover and cook for 1 hour, then cool and transfer to a freezer-proof container. Seal, label and freeze for up to 3 months.

● To serve: thaw overnight in the refrigerator. Reheat at 190C /375F /gas 5 for 50 minutes. Add the mushrooms and cook for 10 minutes. Place in a hot dish and pour the soured cream over it. Sprinkle with parsley.

Pork with port

🍴🍴 30 minutes before freezing, then 1 hour

Serves 4-6
2 fresh pork fillets, trimmed
100 g /4 oz sliced ham, cut in strips
100 g /4 oz Lancashire cheese
5 ml /1 tsp dried thyme
To finish
6 streaky bacon slices, rinded and stretched
500 g /1 lb carrots, pared and sliced
500 g /1 lb leeks, cleaned and sliced
150 ml /5 fl oz tawny port

1 Using a sharp knife, slit the fillets lengthways, almost right through. Open them and beat them gently until they are flattened, taking care not to split them completely in half.
2 Sandwich the ham in the middle of the fillets. Crumble the cheese and thyme over the ham.
3 Roll the fillets up widthways. Tie them with thin string.
4 To freeze: wrap the rolls in a double thickness of freezer foil. Seal, label and freeze for up to 2 months.

● To serve: thaw overnight in the refrigerator. Cut off the string and wrap three slices of bacon around each roll. Secure with cocktail sticks. Make a bed of sliced carrots and leeks in a roasting tin and place the pork rolls on the bed. Pour the port over the rolls and then cook at 190C /375F /gas 5 for 30 minutes. Baste, adding water if necessary, and cook for a further 30 minutes.

Lift out the rolls and slice. Arrange the vegetables on a hot plate with the meat on top and serve.

Gooseberry fool

To purée the gooseberries, do not top and tail them. Simply cook them with 200 g / 5 oz sugar to 500 g / 1 lb fruit and a spoonful or two of water to prevent them from sticking. Then rub them through a sieve. Put the cold purée into containers, leaving a headspace, then cover, label and freeze.

thawing overnight,
then 5 minutes

Serves 4–6
600 ml /1 pt gooseberry purée
275 ml /10 fl oz thick cream
sponge fingers, to serve

1 Thaw the frozen purée overnight in the refrigerator.
2 Whip the cream until it just flops from the whisk and fold it into the purée. Do not blend the cream and purée completely — it looks more attractive if some of the cream is just marbled through the fruit.
3 Turn the fool into a large dish or individual dishes and serve with sponge fingers, if wished.

● To make the gooseberry fool into ice cream, freeze it again when you have blended in the cream. Remember to allow the ice cream to soften in the refrigerator for 45 minutes before serving it.

Freezer peach jam

This peach jam has an excellent flavour and is quick and simple to make.

15 minutes,
then 24 hours standing

Makes about 1 kg /2 lb jam
700 g /1½ lb peaches
900 g /2 lb caster sugar
30 ml /2 tbls lemon juice
125 g /4 fl oz commercial pectin

1 First remove the skins of the peaches: if they are very ripe they will just peel off. If the peaches are under-ripe plunge the fruit in boiling water for 1 minute, remove them, then plunge them into cold water. After this the skins should rub or peel off easily.
2 Stone the peaches. Put the flesh into a bowl and mash it gently.
3 Stir in the sugar and lemon juice and leave it to stand until the sugar has dissolved. Stir occasionally.
4 Add the pectin and stir well for 2–3 minutes. Pack it into small rigid containers, cover and leave at room temperature for 24 hours. Do not expect a firm set — this is more like a conserve. Seal, label carefully and freeze.

● A small container of jam will thaw at room temperature in about 1 hour. Use it to fill cooked pastry shells, to make peach tartlets or to spoon over ice cream. Once thawed, it will keep in a refrigerator for up to a week.

Normandy pork

1¼ hours before freezing,
then 1 hour

Serves 4–6
250 g /8 oz button mushrooms, sliced
½ the fried pork cubes
60 ml /4 tbls brandy
300 ml /10 fl oz dry white wine
To finish
150 ml /5 fl oz thick cream
60 ml /4 tbls chopped fresh parsley

1 Heat the oven to 190C /375F /gas 5. Add the mushrooms to the pork in the casserole.
2 Drain the juices from the casserole into a frying-pan. Add the brandy to the juices, warm slightly and set alight. When the flames die down, add the wine and bring to the boil. Pour the juices over the meat. Cover the casserole and cook in the oven for 1 hour.
3 Allow the casserole to cool. Seal it in a freezer-proof container, label and freeze for up to 3 months.

● To serve: thaw overnight in the refrigerator. Reheat at 190C /375F /gas 5 for 45 minutes. Stir in the cream and parsley. Cook for 15 minutes and serve.

Pork and prunes

soaking the prunes, then 45 minutes
before freezing, then 1¾ hours

Serves 4–6
14 prunes, stoned
150 ml /5 fl oz sherry
2 fresh pork fillets, trimmed
14 juniper berries
25 g /1 oz butter
To finish
15 g /½ oz flour
150 ml /5 fl oz thin cream
30 ml /2 tbls redcurrant jelly

1 Soak the prunes overnight in the sherry mixed with 150 ml /5 fl oz water.
2 Using a sharp knife, slit the fillets lengthways, almost right through. Open them up and beat them until flattened.
3 Drain the prunes, reserving the marinade. Split the prunes open and sandwich them between each fillet. Place a juniper berry on each prune.
4 Roll up along the width. Tie with string. Fry each roll in butter until well browned.

● To freeze: Wrap the fillets in a double thickness of freezer-proof foil. Seal, label and freeze for up to 2 months. Freeze the marinade separately.
● To serve: thaw both in the refrigerator overnight. Place the pork rolls in a roasting tin and pour the marinade sauce over them. Cook at 180C /350F /gas 4 for 1¾ hours. Transfer the rolls to a hot serving dish and put the roasting tin over a moderate heat. Stir in the flour and cook for 1 minute. Add the cream and redcurrant jelly and heat through, without boiling, until thickened. Serve the pork sliced, with the sauce.

Raspberry soufflé

If you want to have a ready-prepared dessert in the freezer, this cold raspberry soufflé is ideal. To freeze extra raspberries for decorating, arrange them in a single layer on a baking tray. Open freeze them until they are solid, then pack them into rigid containers to avoid them being crushed. Cover, label and freeze. Frozen in this way, the raspberries should be free running, allowing you to use only as much as you need.

⏲ 40 minutes, plus cooling,
15 minutes to decorate after thawing

Serves 4
500 g /1 lb raspberries
15 g /½ oz powdered gelatine
3 medium-sized eggs, separated
125 g /4 oz caster sugar
150 ml /5 fl oz thick cream
To decorate after thawing
a few raspberries
150 ml /5 fl oz thick cream

1 Prepare a 15 cm /6 in or 700 ml /1¼ pt soufflé dish by tying a collar of double thickness foil around the outside so that it stands about 5 cm /2 in above the rim.
2 Pick over the raspberries and rub them through a sieve, or blend and then sieve them to remove the seeds.
3 Put 45 ml /3 tbls water into a small bowl, stir in the gelatine and stand the bowl in a pan of hot water until the gelatine has dissolved. Cool slightly, then stir into the raspberry purée.
4 If you own an electric mixer, whisk the egg yolks with the sugar at a high speed until they are thick. Alternatively, put the egg yolks into a bowl with the sugar. Stand the bowl over a pan of hot water and hand whisk until the mixture is thick and creamy. Remove the bowl from the heat and continue to whisk until cool.
5 Stir the purée into the egg yolk mixture. Whip the cream until it begins to thicken and fold it in.
6 Whisk the egg whites until they form stiff peaks. Using a metal spoon, fold them gently into the soufflé mixture. Pour this into the

prepared soufflé dish and leave to set in the refrigerator.
7 Open freeze by standing the soufflé on a baking tray, uncovered, with the collar still in position. When it is hard, slip it into a polythene bag or stand it in a deep rigid container, seal, label and return to the freezer for up to 3 months.

● To serve: thaw the soufflé overnight in the refrigerator, then remove the collar. Prepare a few loose frozen raspberries for decoration. They should not be completely thawed, but allowed to remain slightly frozen so they retain their shape. Whip the cream until it is thick enough to pipe. Now transfer it to a piping bag fitted with a rose or writing nozzle and pipe rosettes around the edge of the soufflé or lattice strips across the top. Decorate with the raspberries and then serve.
● Damaged or over-ripe raspberries can be used to make the purée for this delicious and light soufflé.

Summer fruit for the freezer

Feeding
the Family

NEW WAYS WITH OLD FAVOURITES

Pea and sorrel soup

Boiled chicken and rice
Steamed carrots and green beans

French cherry tart

Plan-ahead timetable

On the day before the meal
Pea and sorrel soup: make but do not add the lemon juice, seasoning or garnish. Store in the refrigerator.
French cherry tart: make the tart and refrigerate.

Two hours before the meal
Boiled chicken and rice: cook the chicken in the oven until it is tender.

This menu plays safe but is delicious at the same time. It is a perfect meal for a family occasion as the recipes are interesting enough to keep more mature palates happy and yet not too highly flavoured or unusual for children. This is not a difficult meal to prepare, and the results will be impressive.

We start with Pea and sorrel soup. For this dish you can use either fresh or frozen peas. I tend to use frozen ones as they are such an enormous time-saver, ideal for when you want to devote attention to your family. The peas are puréed in a blender and then sieved to give a really smooth result. The soup is enriched with thick cream and garnished with crunchy cucumber batons, lightly fried in butter. Strips of sorrel leaves are sprinkled over the top for added flavour.

The main course is a mild dish of Boiled chicken and rice, served with Steamed carrots and green beans. For the best results I like to use an old-fashioned boiling fowl, but not many shops sell them these days and you may have to use a roasting chicken instead. If you do manage to get hold of a genuine boiler — which may turn out to be a bigger bird — extend the cooking time to make sure it is cooked until tender. The smooth, creamy sauce, gently seasoned with black pepper and nutmeg, is made with the stock from cooking the bird and will be perfect with the chicken meat and also complement the delicate vegetables. The baby carrots and fresh green beans are simply steamed and lightly buttered before serving.

Finish the meal with my version of the ever-popular cherry tart. The fruit is placed in a pastry case and covered with a kirsch-flavoured batter. The tart is then cooked for 30 minutes. This is a very convenient dish as it can be prepared and cooked the day before and then refrigerated. Alternatively, put it in the oven to cook while you are having your starter and main course and serve it hot.

Forty minutes before the meal
Boiled chicken and rice: remove the chicken from the casserole and keep it hot. Strain the stock. Cook the rice and make the cream sauce. Keep hot.
Steamed carrots and green beans: prepare, then steam the carrots and green beans.

Just before the meal
Pea and sorrel soup: add the lemon juice and seasonings, garnish and serve.

Between the first and the main course
Boiled chicken and rice: place the chicken in the centre of a large heated serving platter and surround it with mounds of rice. Pour the sauce over the chicken.
Steamed carrots and green beans: toss the carrots in lemon juice and butter. Toss the green beans in butter, season with salt and black pepper and serve.

Between the main course and the dessert
French cherry tart: sprinkle with icing sugar and serve.

Pea and sorrel soup

Serves 4–6
50 g /2 oz butter
700 g /1½ lb peas, defrosted if frozen
1.1 L /2 pt chicken stock, home-made or from cubes
1 cucumber, peeled, to garnish
2 egg yolks
150 ml /5 fl oz thick cream
10 ml /2 tsp lemon juice
salt and freshly ground black pepper
cayenne pepper
6–8 sorrel leaves, cut into narrow strips

1 Melt 25 g /1 oz of the butter in a medium-sized saucepan and add the peas and 30 ml /2 tbls chicken stock. Cover and cook the peas, stirring occasionally, until cooked through.
2 Reserve one-third of the peas for the garnish. Purée the other two-thirds in a blender with half the remaining stock. Sieve the purée.
3 For the garnish, cut the peeled cucumber into 4 cm /1½ in lengths. Halve them and remove the seeds. Now cut the flesh into small sticks. In a small pan, simmer these cucumber batons in the remaining butter until they are tender, about 3 minutes. Remove with a slotted spoon and reserve for the garnish.
4 Beat the egg yolks with the thick cream. Mix them well and add them to the pea purée.
5 Bring the remaining stock to the boil, remove from the heat and stir in the purée mixture. Return to the heat and cook over a gentle heat, stirring continuously, until the soup is smooth and thick. Do not let it come to the boil or it will curdle.
6 Just before serving, add the lemon juice, salt and freshly ground black pepper, and a pinch of cayenne pepper. Garnish with the reserved peas, cucumber batons and strips of sorrel leaves.

45 minutes

Boiled chicken and rice

Serves 4–6
1.4 kg /3 lb chicken, dressed weight
1 Spanish onion, stuck with 2 cloves
2 large carrots, quartered
bouquet garni
2 celery sticks, coarsely chopped
175 ml /6 fl oz dry white wine
1.1 L /2 pt chicken stock, home-made or from cubes
salt
black peppercorns
15 g /½ oz butter
1 Spanish onion, finely chopped
225 g /8 oz long-grain rice
freshly ground black pepper
For the cream sauce
25 g /1 oz butter
30 ml /2 tbls flour
450 ml /15 fl oz thick cream
salt
freshly ground white pepper
freshly grated nutmeg

1 Place the chicken in a flameproof casserole with the onion stuck with cloves, the quartered carrots, the bouquet garni and the coarsely chopped celery. Pour in the dry white wine and the chicken stock, season with salt and add a few black peppercorns. Simmer gently for about 1–1½ hours, or until the chicken is tender. Remove the chicken from the casserole and keep it hot. Strain the stock and reserve.
2 Melt the butter in a saucepan. Add the finely chopped Spanish onion and cook over a gentle heat for 4–5 minutes, or until it is translucent, stirring occasionally with a wooden spoon.
3 Stir in the rice, 275 ml /10 fl oz of the reserved chicken stock and 575 ml /1 pt hot water. Season to taste with salt and freshly ground black pepper, bring to the boil, then stir to dislodge any grains of rice stuck to the pan. Reduce the heat, cover and simmer gently for 15–25 minutes, or until the rice is tender but not mushy.
4 Meanwhile, make the cream sauce. Melt the butter in a heavy-based saucepan. When it begins to bubble, add the flour, blend with a wooden spoon and continue stirring over a low heat for 2–3 minutes, to make a pale roux.
5 Gradually add 150 ml /5 fl oz strained chicken stock and the thick cream, stirring vigorously with a wire whisk to prevent lumps forming. Bring the sauce to the boil, stirring continuously, then reduce the heat and simmer for 5–10 minutes or until the sauce is thick and smooth, stirring occasionally. Season to taste with salt and freshly ground white pepper, and freshly grated nutmeg.

● Serve the chicken on a warm platter with the rice and cream sauce. You can either serve the Steamed carrots and green beans separately, or on the same dish.

2 hours

Steamed carrots and green beans

Serves 4–6

350 g /12 oz baby carrots, peeled
350 g /12 oz green beans, topped and tailed
10 ml /2 tsp lemon juice
25 g /1 oz butter
salt and freshly ground black pepper

1 Place the peeled baby carrots in a steamer or metal colander over a saucepan of simmering water. Cover tightly and steam for 5 minutes.
2 Push the carrots to one side and add the prepared green beans. Cover again and steam for a further 15 minutes, or until the vegetables are tender.
3 Place the carrots in a small bowl. Pour in the lemon juice, add half the butter and toss until the butter has melted and the carrots are well coated. Now season to taste with salt and freshly ground black pepper.
4 Place the green beans in another bowl, toss with the remaining butter and season with salt and freshly ground black pepper to taste. Arrange attractively on a heated serving platter and serve.

35 minutes

French cherry tart

Serves 4–6

350 g /12 oz made-weight shortcrust pastry, defrosted if frozen
flour, for dusting
For the filling
275 ml /10 fl oz milk
½ vanilla pod
60 ml /4 tbls caster sugar
15 ml /1 tbls kirsch
15 ml /1 tbls flour
15 ml /1 tbls cornflour
1 egg, beaten
350 g /12 oz red cherries
icing sugar, to decorate

1 Roll out the pastry 3–6 mm /⅛–¼ in thick on a lightly floured surface. Lift the pastry on the rolling pin over a 24 cm /9½ in flan tin and unroll.
2 Press the pastry into the tin from the base outwards, being careful not to stretch it as it will shrink back later. Trim away any excess pastry by rolling with the pin across the top. Prick the base with a fork and chill the pastry case for 30 minutes.
3 Heat the oven and a baking sheet to 200C /400F /gas 6. Line the pastry case with foil and beans. Bake it on the sheet for 10 minutes.
4 Turn the oven down to 180C /350F /gas 4. Remove the foil and beans and bake the case for a further 8 minutes. Remove it from the oven and leave it to cool in its tin on the baking sheet. Leave the oven on at the same setting.
5 To make the filling, pour the milk into the top pan of a double boiler. Split the vanilla pod and add it to the milk with the caster sugar and the kirsch. Bring to the boil, then remove from the heat.
6 Sift the flour and cornflour into a bowl. Make a well in the centre and pour in the beaten egg. Beat with a whisk, drawing in the flours, and whisk into a smooth batter.
7 Gradually strain the hot milk into the batter, stirring with a wooden spoon. Return the mixture to the top pan of the double boiler and cook for 1 minute over simmering water. Leave to cool.
8 Wash the cherries and remove the stalks and stones.
9 Line the pastry case with the cherries. Pour in the batter and bake in the oven for 30 minutes.
10 Remove the tart from the tin. Sprinkle with icing sugar and serve.

 1¾ hours,
including chilling the pastry

A WEEKEND TREAT

Citrus cocktail

~

Aromatic roast pork
Mixed vegetable salad
Glazed carrots

~

Gâteau mocha

Plan-ahead timetable

On the day before the meal
Gâteau mocha: make the two gateau layers and store them in an airtight container. Toast the almonds.

On the morning of the meal
Gâteau mocha: make the filling, assemble and chill.

Five and a half hours before the meal
Citrus cocktail: make the paste for the Bohemian dressing.
Aromatic roast pork: make the herb flavouring and stuff the pork. Leave it to marinate.
Mixed vegetable salad: prepare and cook the cauliflower, broccoli and French beans, then add the dressing. Leave the salad to go cold.

There are occasions when you have to feed the family but you want to experiment with some slightly more unusual, sophisticated and special dishes — times like Saturday evening when aunts and uncles or grandparents are visiting or when friends are staying and will eat with you and the children.

In this chapter I suggest three dishes which are enjoyable to cook and which can be adapted for children if necessary. The first course, Citrus cocktail with a Bohemian dressing, is optional since children do not always want a starter and may dislike the oil and vinegar dressing. You could make enough just to serve the adults, and give the children half a grapefruit each.

The Citrus cocktail provides a complementary, acidic contrast to the main course which is Aromatic roast pork, a simple home-cooked dish presented in a new way. When cooked and carved, the pork has a beautiful marbled appearance due to the special blend of aromatic herbs — fennel, chives and garlic — which turns this joint into sensational eating. Serve the roast with sweetened Glazed carrots which are garnished with dill sprigs and a Mixed vegetable salad. These two dishes with their array of colours will give eye-catching appeal to the meal. Add some roast potatoes for the children if desired and if you feel they will prefer their salad without a dressing you could serve their portions in a separate bowl with just a knob of butter on the top. Alternatively, you could serve them just potatoes and carrots with their meat.

For the finale, I suggest a rich coffee butter cream cake. Gâteau mocha can look as simple or as splendid as you like. Pipe extra coffee cream on the top if you wish. Personally I like to chill the cake for several hours before serving it. Accompanied by a good bottle of white wine for the adults — I suggest a Riesling — these three courses will create a special meal which everyone will remember!

One and three-quarter hours before the meal
Aromatic roast pork: drain, tie, sear and roast the pork.
Mixed vegetable salad: prepare the remaining vegetables.
Glazed carrots with dill seeds: prepare the carrots.
Citrus cocktail: prepare the ingredients.

Twenty-five minutes before the meal
Mixed vegetable salad: add the tomatoes, cucumber and
celery to the salad. Transfer to a serving dish and chill.
Aromatic roast pork: turn up the oven, drain off the excess
fat, add the reserved marinade and finish cooking.
Glazed carrots: simmer the carrots.

Just before the meal
Citrus cocktail: add the oil to the dressing. Sprinkle over the
cocktail.

Citrus cocktail

Serves 6
1 Cos lettuce
2 bunches watercress
3 oranges
2 grapefruit
1 lime
For the Bohemian dressing
2.5 ml /½ tsp dry mustard
2.5 ml /½ tsp salt
1.5 ml /¼ tsp caster sugar
45 ml /3 tbls tarragon vinegar
5 ml /1 tsp finely chopped shallot
5 ml /1 tsp finely chopped fresh parsley
2.5 ml /½ tsp finely chopped fresh tarragon
1 garlic clove, lightly crushed
135 ml /9 tbls olive oil

1 To make the Bohemian dressing, in a bowl, blend the mustard,
salt, caster sugar and tarragon vinegar to a smooth paste. Stir in the
finely chopped shallot, parsley and tarragon and lightly crushed
garlic. Leave for at least 1 hour.
2 Wash the lettuce and carefully dry each leaf. Cut the lettuce
coarsely across the grain and arrange it in a glass dish. Wash the
watercress and cut away the stalks. Make a border of the leaves
around the outer edge of the dish.
3 Peel the oranges, removing all the pith, and cut them into
segments with a sharp knife. Carefully remove all pips with the point
of the knife. Repeat with the grapefruit. Arrange the orange and
grapefruit segments in the centre of the dish of salad greens. Remove
the crushed garlic from the dressing and add the olive oil 15 ml /
1 tbls at a time, beating with a fork until the dressing emulsifies.
Sprinkle it over the salad.
4 Slice the lime thinly and make a cut to the centre of each slice.
Twist the slices and then arrange them around the watercress border
at the edge of the dish.

1½ hours

Aromatic roast pork

Serves 6

1.1–1.4 kg /2½–3 lb boned loin of
pork, with all but a thin
sheet of surface fat removed
60 ml /4 tbls olive oil
150 ml /5 fl oz dry white wine
salt and ground black pepper
25 g /1 oz butter
fennel leaves, to garnish

**For the aromatic herb
flavouring**
20 sprigs fennel, finely
chopped
30 ml /2 tbls finely snipped fresh
chives
4 garlic cloves, chopped
2.5 ml /½ tsp coarse salt

1   To make the aromatic herb flavouring, combine the chopped
fennel, snipped chives and chopped garlic in a small bowl. Add the
coarse salt and mix well.
2   Wipe the untied meat and, with the point of a sharp knife or a
metal skewer, pierce the loin of pork deeply in 12 places. Force
generous amounts of the aromatic herb flavouring into these holes in
sufficient quantity so that the roast will be marbled with colour when
it is carved.
3   Rub the joint with olive oil and sprinkle it with the remaining
herb flavouring. Place the joint in a bowl and add the dry white wine.
Cover the bowl loosely with foil and marinate the pork in a cool place
for 3–4 hours, turning the meat several times to absorb the flavours.
4   When ready to roast the meat, remove the pork from the marinade
juices and allow it to drain thoroughly. Reserve the marinade and pat
the meat dry. Weigh the stuffed meat and calculate the cooking time,
allowing 35–40 minutes per kg /16–18 minutes per lb.
5   Heat the oven to 170C /325F /gas 3. Season the meat generously
with salt and freshly ground black pepper. Roll up the joint and tie it
in 4 or 5 places with string.
6   Heat the butter in a small flameproof roasting pan, and sear the
meat on all sides.
7   Place the joint on a rack in the roasting pan in the oven and roast
the pork for 20 minutes less than the calculated cooking time.
8   Remove the meat from the oven and increase the oven
temperature to 220C /425F /gas 7. Drain off the excess fat from the
pan and add the reserved marinade juice. Return to the oven and
cook for another 20 minutes.
9   Transfer the joint to a warmed serving dish and remove the string.
Leave it in the turned-off oven while you make the gravy. Add 150
ml / 5 fl oz water to the pan juices, bring to a gentle boil, adjust the
seasoning and strain into a warm jug. Skim off all excess fat and serve
with the roast pork. Garnish the pork with fennel leaves.

 30 minutes, plus 3–4 hours marinating,
then 1¾ hours

Mixed vegetable salad

Serves 6

salt
½ cauliflower, weighing about
250 g /8 oz
175 g /6 oz large broccoli heads
100 g /4 oz French beans
250 g /8 oz medium-sized
tomatoes
½ cucumber
2 celery sticks

For the dressing
30 ml /2 tbls wine vinegar
salt and freshly ground pepper
lemon juice
1 garlic clove, finely chopped
90–120 ml /6–8 tbls olive oil
30 ml /2 tbls finely chopped
fresh parsley
30 ml /2 tbls finely snipped fresh
chives, or spring onion tops

1   Put a large saucepan of salted water on to boil.
2   Meanwhile, start preparing the vegetables. Break the cauliflower
into florets measuring about 4 cm /1½ in in diameter, cutting away
any hard stalks (do not cut off too much or the florets will fall apart),
and rinse in cold water. Cut away any stalks and large leaves from
the broccoli, then rinse in cold water. Top, tail and then rinse the
French beans.
3   When the water is boiling gently, add the cauliflower florets,
broccoli and the green beans and cook for 5 minutes.
4   While the vegetables are cooking, make the dressing. In a bowl,
combine the wine vinegar with a generous seasoning of salt and
freshly ground black pepper and lemon juice to taste. Add the finely
chopped garlic and, with a fork, gradually beat in the olive oil until
the dressing thickens and emulsifies. Stir in the finely chopped
parsley and snipped chives, or spring onion tops.
5   When the vegetables are cooked (they should still be fairly crisp),
drain them thoroughly, and place them in a bowl. While they are still
warm, pour the dressing over the vegetables. Toss them carefully,
using your hands or a large spoon, and taking care not to break the
florets or broccoli sprigs.
6   Blanch, skin and seed the tomatoes, and cut each one into 8
wedges. Peel the cucumber and quarter it lengthways, remove the
cucumber seeds and cut the flesh into 25 mm /1 in lengths. Clean the
celery and cut into 25 mm /1 in slices.
7   Add the tomato wedges, cucumber and celery slices to the dressed
vegetables and toss carefully. Transfer the salad to a serving dish.

● On another occasion, sliced cooked carrots could be included in
this dish for extra colour.

 1½ hours,
including cooling

Glazed carrots

Serves 6
700 g /1½ lb small carrots
75 g /3 oz butter
90 ml /6 tbls chicken stock, home-made or from a cube
15–30 ml /1–2 tbls sugar
2.5–5 ml /½–1 tsp dill seeds, crushed
salt and freshly ground black pepper
butter, for greasing
4–6 sprigs dill

1 Scrape or peel the carrots and slice them thinly. Rinse and pat them dry.
2 Place the carrots in a heavy saucepan with the butter, chicken stock and sugar and crushed dill seeds to taste. Season with salt and freshly ground black pepper to taste.
3 Cover the carrots with a piece of buttered paper and simmer gently for about 30 minutes, until the carrots are tender and the liquid has almost completely evaporated. The carrots should be glazed but take care they do not dry out and burn.
4 Give the carrots a light toss and turn them out onto a heated serving dish. Garnish with sprigs of fresh dill and serve immediately.

 45 minutes

Gâteau mocha

Serves 6
37 ml /2½ tbls melted butter
100 g /4 oz flour, plus 15 ml / 1 tbls for dusting
5 eggs
100 g /4 oz sugar
For the filling
225 g /8 oz unsalted butter
15 ml /1 tbls coffee essence, mixed with 15 ml /1 tbls hot water
225 g /8 oz sugar
4 egg yolks
For the decoration
50–75 g /2–3 oz almonds, chopped and toasted
icing sugar

1 Heat the oven to 180C /350F /gas 4. Using 7 ml /½ tbls of the melted butter, grease two 23 cm /8 in sandwich cake tins. Line the bases with 23 cm /8 in circles of greaseproof or waxed paper. Using another 7 ml /½ tbls melted butter, grease the paper. Dust the tins with 15 ml /1 tbls flour, shaking out any excess.
2 In a large heatproof mixing bowl, whisk the eggs until pale. Add the sugar and place the bowl over a pan of boiling water. Whisk the egg mixture until it is thick and pale and leaves a ribbon trail. Remove bowl from the pan; continue whisking until mixture is cool.
3 Sift the remaining flour onto the egg mixture and gently fold it in with a metal spoon. Fold in the remaining melted butter, a little at a time. Pour the batter into the tins and carefully tip the tins so that the batter is smooth on top. Bake in the centre of the oven for 15–20 minutes, or until the cakes have risen and are golden.
4 Turn the cakes out onto a wire rack to cool. Remove the paper and leave the cakes until they are cold.
5 To make the filling, cream the butter with a wooden spoon until it is light and fluffy. Beat in the coffee liquid. Set aside.
6 Dissolve the sugar in 50 ml /2 fl oz water over a moderate heat, stirring constantly. Bring the mixture to the boil. Without stirring, continue boiling the syrup until it reaches 100C /215F on a sugar thermometer; at this temperature a small amount dropped into cold water forms a short thread when pulled between two spoons.
7 Meanwhile, whisk the egg yolks until pale and thick. Whisking constantly, add the hot syrup, a little at a time, and continue whisking until the mixture is very thick and smooth. Continue to whisk until the mixture is cool. Now whisk the butter and coffee mixture into the egg mixture, a little at a time, until well blended.
8 Place one cake on a serving dish and spread it with one-third of the filling. Place the second cake on top and cover with another one-third of the filling. Cover the sides of the cake with the remainder and sprinkle the chopped almonds over the top and the sides of the cake. Sift icing sugar over the top. Chill or serve immediately.

2½ hours, plus cooling (and chilling if wished)

SOMETHING FOR EVERYONE

Egg mayonnaise with cucumber and tomatoes

Gammon steaks with apple stuffing
Country-style green beans
Swiss potato cake

Cold raspberry mousse

Here is a really easy-to-make meal for a family of four. Most people, even fussy children, like eggs, so the starter for this meal will be popular. An ordinary egg mayonnaise is turned into something special by the addition of chopped tomatoes, cucumber and black olives which add a dramatic touch to the dish.

Follow the Egg mayonnaise with Gammon steaks and apple stuffing, where the tangy fruit filling offsets the richness of the gammon steaks. With the steaks serve Country-style green beans, beans cooked until they are tender but still crisp, combined with baby carrots and button onions simmered in a chicken stock. Strips of sautéed bacon may be added to the vegetables if wished and the whole

Plan-ahead timetable

Three hours before the meal
Cold raspberry mousse: make the mousse and chill it.
Country-style green beans: prepare the beans. Prepare the carrots, peel the onions, cut the bacon into strips, if using.

Two hours before the meal
Gammon steaks with apple stuffing: make the stuffing.
Swiss potato cake: scrub the potatoes, cook and cool.

One and a half hours before the meal
Swiss potato cake: peel, grate the potatoes; mix the cake.
Gammon steaks with apple stuffing: bake the gammon, basting frequently.

Forty minutes before the meal
Swiss potato cake: cook and reserve in the oven.
Egg mayonnaise with cucumber and tomatoes: hard-boil eggs and cool.
Country-style green beans: sauté the bacon, if using, and reserve. Simmer the stock, sugar, carrots, onions. Set aside.

Fifteen minutes before the meal
Egg mayonnaise with cucumber and tomatoes: shell and slice the hard-boiled eggs. Prepare the cucumber and tomatoes. Make the vinaigrette, spoon over and serve.

Between the first and the main course
Country-style green beans: heat the beans, carrots, onion and bacon, if using; stir in the cream, season and garnish.
Gammon steaks with apple stuffing: fry the apple rings, garnish the gammon and serve.
Swiss potato cake: cut into wedges and serve.

dish is then tossed in cream at the last moment for a very luxurious finish.

As a change, for the potato element in the meal try Swiss potato cake. This is also called *rösti* and is a savoury and crunchy addition to the rest of the menu. The younger members of the family may not be alone in asking for second helpings of this! Finish the dinner with a cool, fresh pink-coloured raspberry mousse. It can be made with frozen raspberries but if fresh ones are available, then so much the better. Serve it simply with chilled whipped cream or with a rich vanilla ice cream if preferred.

If you feel like including a wine with this menu, then I suggest that you try a Côtes-du-Rhone, which is a wine to suit most palates.

From the start of the meal — the Egg mayonnaise — to the finish — the Cold raspberry mouse — there is nothing particularly difficult to prepare, and the resulting dishes should be enjoyed by everyone.

Egg mayonnaise with cucumber and tomatoes

Serves 4
6 hard-boiled eggs
300 ml /11 fl oz mayonnaise
½ cucumber
salt
freshly ground black pepper
4 ripe tomatoes, blanched, skinned, seeded and diced
7.5 ml /½ tbls finely chopped fresh tarragon
50 ml /2 fl oz vinaigrette
4 black olives, halved and stoned, to garnish (optional)

1 Shell the hard-boiled eggs and cut them across into even rings.
2 On a large round serving dish, leaving 4 cm /1½ in clear around the edge of the dish, spread a generous circle of mayonnaise, using a palette knife to smooth the surface. Arrange overlapping egg slices over the bed of mayonnaise.
3 Cut the cucumber in half lengthways and remove the seeds with a sharp teaspoon. Cut the halved cucumber into small dice and transfer it to a bowl. Season to taste with salt and freshly ground black pepper. Put the prepared tomatoes in another bowl and season to taste with salt and freshly ground black pepper.
4 Arrange 4 clusters each of diced cucumber and tomatoes alternately around the edge of the dish.
5 Beat the chopped tarragon into the vinaigrette and spoon a little dressing over each vegetable cluster. Arrange 2 halved olives on top of each tomato cluster if wished. Serve immediately.

10 minutes

Gammon steaks with apple stuffing

Serves 4

175 g /6 oz fresh white breadcrumbs
100 g /4 oz seedless raisins
50 g /2 oz peanuts, coarsely chopped
30 ml /2 tbls golden syrup
5 ml /1 tsp dry mustard
90 ml /6 tbls melted butter

4 dessert apples
2 slices gammon, 10 mm /½ in
   thick, weighing 225 g /8 oz each
freshly ground black pepper
4–6 cloves
juice of ½ lemon
30 ml /2 tbls caster sugar

1 Heat the oven to 180C /350F /gas 4. In a bowl combine the fresh breadcrumbs, raisins, coarsely chopped peanuts, golden syrup and dry mustard with 30 ml /2 tbls of the melted butter and mix well.
2 Core and coarsely chop 1 apple and add it to the breadcrumb mixture.
3 With a sharp knife, slit the fat around the gammon steaks at 25 mm / 1 in intervals to prevent them from curling up during cooking. Now season the steaks on both sides with freshly ground black pepper to taste.
4 Grease a shallow baking dish large enough to take 1 gammon steak with 15 ml /1 tbls of the melted butter. Place 1 gammon steak in the prepared dish and pile the stuffing on top, pressing down very gently with the palm of your hand. Place the second gammon steak on top of the stuffing and carefully stick the cloves into the fat around the gammon steaks.
5 Pour 15 ml /1 tbls melted butter over the stuffed gammon and bake in the oven for 1 hour or until the gammon is cooked. Baste frequently during cooking with the juices in the baking dish.
6 Meanwhile, core the remaining apples and cut into 5 mm /¼ in rings. Soak the apple rings in water acidulated with the lemon juice, to prevent discoloration.
7 Lay the prepared apple rings on absorbent paper to drain. Sprinkle the rings on both sides with caster sugar. Heat the remaining melted butter in a large frying-pan and fry the apple rings for 1–2 minutes on each side until they are golden.
8 Transfer the gammon onto a heated platter and garnish with the apple rings. Serve immediately.

 1½ hours

Country-style green beans

Serves 4

700 g /1½ lb young green beans
salt
4 baby carrots, or 2 large carrots
12 small button onions
100 g /4 oz smoked steaky bacon, sliced (optional)
15 g /½ oz butter
90 ml /6 tbls chicken stock, home-made or from a cube
30 ml /2 bls caster sugar
45 ml /3 tbls thick cream
freshly ground black pepper
15 ml /1 tbls finely chopped fresh chervil
15 ml /1 tbls finely chopped fresh parsley

1 Trim and wash the beans, and cut them into 5 cm /2 in lengths. Cook them in a large pan of boiling, salted water, uncovered, for 3–4 minutes, or until the beans are tender but still firm. Drain and refresh them under cold running water.
2 Peel or scrape the carrots. If using baby carrots, cut them into thirds; if using larger carrots, slice them thickly. Now peel the button onions.
3 Cut the bacon into strips, if using. Melt the butter in a pan and sauté the bacon until crisp and golden; remove it with a slotted spoon and keep it warm.
4 In a saucepan, simmer the chicken stock, caster sugar, carrots and button onions together for 10 minutes, or until the carrots and onions are tender but still firm.
5 Toss the green beans, carrots, onion and bacon strips, if using, in cream over a low heat for 1–2 minutes to reheat. Adjust the seasoning and serve in a heated serving dish, sprinkled with the finely chopped chervil and parsley.

30 minutes

Swiss potato cake

Serves 4

750 g /1½ lb medium-sized floury potatoes
salt
25 g /1 oz butter
1 Spanish onion, very finely chopped
freshly ground black pepper
30 ml /2 tbls olive oil

1 Using a stiff brush, scrub the potatoes clean under cold running water.
2 Put the cleaned potatoes in a large saucepan, pour in enough cold water to cover them and add a large pinch of salt. Bring the water to the boil, reduce the heat and simmer the potatoes for 15 minutes until they are three-quarters cooked.
3 Remove the pan from the heat, cover the potatoes and leave for 15 minutes.
4 Drain the potatoes in a colander and cool them under cold running water. When the potatoes are cool enough to handle, slip off the skins with your fingers.
5 Using the large holes on your grater, coarsely grate the potatoes into a large bowl. Cut half the butter into flakes and add them to the bowl with the finely chopped onion. Season generously with salt and freshly ground black pepper. Toss lightly with a large fork to mix the ingredients together without crushing them.
6 Select a heavy-based frying-pan measuring 23 cm /9 in across the base. Heat the olive oil with the remaining butter in the pan. When the fat is quite hot, add the grated potato mixture. Using a spatula or fish slice, lightly pat the mixture into a round cake. Do not compress the mixture too much or the steam will not be able to escape and the cake will be soggy.
7 Fry the potato cake over a low heat for about 15 minutes, until the underside is crusty and well browned. Shake the pan from time to time during cooking to make sure the cake does not stick to the pan.
8 Heat a flat plate which is slightly larger in diameter than the frying-pan.
9 When the underside of the potato cake is cooked, turn out the cake onto the heated plate and quickly slip it straight back into the frying-pan. Fry gently for a further 10–15 minutes until the second side is crisp and well-browned.
10 Turn it out onto a heated serving dish. Serve cut into wedges like a cake.

 1½ hours

Cold raspberry mousse

Serves 4

450 g /1 lb fresh raspberries, or frozen raspberries, thawed and drained
150 g /5 oz caster sugar
15 ml /1 tbls lemon juice
40 g /1½ oz cornflour
1 egg, separated
oil, for greasing
150 ml /5 fl oz thick cream
whipped cream, to garnish and serve

1 If you are using fresh raspberries, reserve a few for decoration. Place the raspberries in a pan with the sugar and 90 ml /6 tbls water. Cook very gently, stirring constantly, until the fruit is soft. Add the lemon juice, then rub the mixture through a fine sieve.
2 Blend the cornflour with 150 ml /5 fl oz water. Stir in the raspberry purée and the egg yolk and mix well.
3 Pour the mixture into a clean saucepan and cook over a very low heat for about 10 minutes, stirring constantly, until it has thickened and no longer tastes of cornflour. Remove the pan from the heat and allow the mixture to cool.
4 Oil a 600 ml /1 pt jelly mould. Whisk the egg white until stiff but not dry. Whisk the thick cream until it holds its shape in soft peaks. Fold the whipped cream into the cooled mousse mixture, followed by the whisked egg white. Pour the mixture into the oiled mould and refrigerate for about 2 hours until it sets.
5 To unmould the mousse, insert the tip of a sharp knife around the edge of the mousse. Hold a hot, damp tea-towel around the mould for 1–2 seconds, then place a lightly wetted plate upside-down on the mould. Invert, give a few shakes and lift off the mould. Garnish with whipped cream and the reserved fresh raspberries, if used, and serve with chilled whipped cream.

● This lovely, simple pudding can also be made with blackcurrants or peeled, sliced peaches.

 40 minutes,
plus chilling

HEARTY FOOD FOR ALL

When the family is home for dinner one evening, this is a good menu to prepare and cook for them. I suggest starting with Seafood cocktail using shrimps, prawns, crab meat or a luxurious combination of all three. This can be made in advance, though it will take very little time to assemble at the last minute. If the younger members of the family prefer not to have a starter, then they can easily fill up with one of the two delicious desserts served at the end of the meal.

Preparing the casserole the day before is a way of making life much easier for yourself, apart from the fact that it helps to improve its flavour if it is left for 24 hours or so because the ingredients have time to blend together and mature. If you do this, you will be able to chill the casserole so that you can remove any congealed fat from the surface before you reheat it.

Try serving Crunchy noodles as a change from the usual potatoes. Not only is there no tedious potato peeling, but the dish can be ready in only 15 minutes. Tangy sautéed courgettes offer a contrast of flavour and texture to suit most people's tastes.

End the meal with my delicious fresh Fruit medley, which is based on a recipe from Imperial Russia. If the family meal is to be a celebration or a special occasion, then the fresh Fruit medley can be made with a sweet champagne or a sparkling white wine to replace the fruit juice and this makes it a much richer dessert. For the children —

or any adult with a sweet tooth — try a Chocolate banana pie as an alternative. This is a popular American recipe for a sweet tart with a frothy layer of orange chiffon on top. The orange flavour can be enhanced by the addition of Grand Marnier, if you wish.

If you want a simpler family dinner, however, centre your meal on the casserole. Prepare it during the morning of the day you require it and then just pop it in the oven 35 minutes before you intend to eat. Forget about a starter or even cooking vegetables! Fill out the meal with French bread (spread with garlic butter, wrapped in foil and then heated through in the oven). To keep your preparations to the absolute minimum, serve just a simple salad with the casserole and then a cheese board or fresh fruit for dessert. These suggestions mean that your main course is wonderfully flexible and that you could easily serve double the numbers you had originally planned for — if, for instance, someone brings home unexpected guests.

Should you decide to have a bottle of wine with the meal, then choose a Barolo, which is a full-bodied red wine from Italy, or a beaujolais. Either of these will go well with the casserole because this substantial dish is suited to robust red wine.

Whichever decision you make, whether to serve a full menu or just to concentrate on the casserole, you will have a truly delicious dinner with very little fuss and bother that will be enjoyed by all the family. What more could any cook ask for?

Seafood cocktail

Casserole of beef

Crunchy noodles

Tangy sautéed courgettes

Fruit medley
or
Chocolate banana pie

Plan-ahead timetable

On the day before the meal
Casserole of beef: make the casserole and cool it.
Chocolate banana pie: make the pastry case and bake it.

Three hours before the meal
Chocolate banana pie: make the filling. Chill until set.

Two hours before the meal
Fruit medley: prepare the fruit. Leave to macerate with the vanilla sugar.

One hour before the meal
Fruit medley: add the fruit juice to the salad and chill.
Crunchy noodles: blanch and slice the almonds.
Chocolate banana pie: assemble and then refrigerate.

Thirty-five minutes before the meal
Casserole of beef: heat the oven to 180C /350F /gas 4.
Scrape any fat off the top. Put the covered casserole into heat. Warm the plates and vegetable dishes.
Tangy sautéed courgettes: sauté the courgettes and make the onion and tomato mixture. Assemble and keep warm.

Twenty minutes before the meal
Crunchy noodles: put the noodles onto boil and cook the topping. Combine the two and keep warm.
Seafood cocktail: prepare the ingredients. Assemble.

Five minutes before the meal
Casserole of beef: glaze the onions and add to the casserole. Return to the oven during the first course.

Between the first and the main course
Crunchy noodles: toss before serving.
Chocolate banana pie: remove from refrigerator and decorate.
Casserole of beef: remove from the oven and serve.

Seafood cocktail

Serves 4
1 lettuce
175 g /6 oz peeled shrimps or prawns or flaked canned crabmeat
paprika
4 lemon wedges
freshly snipped chives, to garnish
4 whole prawns, unpeeled, to garnish
4 sprigs of parsley, to garnish
For the dressing
250 ml /9 fl oz thick mayonnaise
5 ml /1 tsp French mustard
5 ml /1 tsp lemon juice
45 ml /3 tbls tomato ketchup
a dash of Worcestershire sauce
a dash of Tabasco sauce
salt and freshly ground black pepper

1 To make the dressing, combine the mayonnaise with the French mustard and lemon juice. Blend in the tomato ketchup and flavour to taste with the Worcestershire sauce and Tabasco sauce. Adjust the seasoning if necessary and chill.
2 Wash and dry the lettuce very carefully. Shred it finely.
3 To assemble, half-fill 4 decorative dishes with the lettuce. Now divide the seafood among the glasses. Spoon the dressing over each portion. Dust with paprika.
4 Dip the edge of each lemon wedge into the paprika and serve one with each cocktail.
5 Garnish each serving with the fresh chives, a whole prawn and a sprig of parsley.

● Try using a mixture of two or more of the seafoods listed in the ingredients, if you prefer.

 15 minutes

Casserole of beef

Serves 4
2 Spanish onions, finely chopped
4 garlic cloves, finely chopped
3 shallots, finely chopped
275 g /10 oz piece of green bacon
  or ham, cut into strips
25 g /1 oz butter
125 g /4 oz piece of pork rind
1 kg /2 lb lean braising beef
salt
freshly ground black pepper
bouquet garni
1 small onion, stuck with 1 clove
a pinch of allspice
700 ml /25 fl oz beef stock, home-
  made or from a cube
25 g /1 oz beurre manié (12 g /
  ½ oz butter mashed with 12 g /
  ½ oz flour)
75 ml /5 tbls tomato purée
24 button onions, glazed, to
  garnish (see note below)

1 In a bowl, combine the onions with the garlic, shallots and strips of bacon or ham. Grease the base of a heavy 3 L /5 pt flameproof casserole with butter and place the piece of pork rind on top, skin side up.
2 Cut the beef into 3 cm /1½ in cubes, trimming away any pieces of fat or gristle. Put a layer of cubes on top of the pork rind and season with salt and pepper. Sprinkle with a little of the onion mixture. Continue layering the ingredients until they are all used up, then bury the bouquet garni and the whole onion in the centre. Sprinkle with salt, pepper and allspice.
3 Heat the oven to 120C /250F /gas ½. Pour the stock into the casserole. Cover and heat slowly so that it takes about 20 minutes to reach boiling point.
4 Skim the surface, removing any froth or impurities. Cover the casserole tightly, transfer it to the oven and bake for 2½–3 hours.
5 Remove the casserole from the oven and discard the piece of pork rind, the bouquet garni and the whole onion. Stir the *beurre manié*, in tiny pieces into the sauce, together with the tomato purée, and then simmer gently until the sauce has thickened and no longer tastes of flour.
6 Add the glazed button onions and simmer a few minutes longer.

● To glaze the button onions for garnishing, fry them in butter over a low heat. Sprinkle a little soft brown sugar over them just before the end of the cooking time and shake the pan well to coat the onions thoroughly.
● To turn this dish into a dinner party recipe, replace the beef stock with a bottle of red wine.

3¼ hours

Crunchy noodles

Serves 4
350 g /12 oz ribbon noodles
salt
50 g /2 oz butter
50 g /2 oz almonds, blanched and thinly sliced
50 g /2 oz fresh white breadcrumbs
freshly ground black pepper

1 Simmer the noodles in salted water until cooked but still firm when tested. This will take 10–12 minutes. Drain thoroughly in a colander. Place in a deep, heated serving dish and keep hot.
2 While the noodles are cooking, melt the butter in a saucepan and toss the almonds and breadcrumbs in it. Sauté gently until crisp and golden in colour.
3 Top the noodles with the buttered almond and breadcrumb mixture. Season to taste with salt and freshly ground black pepper. Just before serving, toss the noodles gently to distribute the almond and crumb mixture.

15 minutes

Tangy sautéed courgettes

Serves 4
700 g /1½ lb small courgettes
60 ml /4 tbls flour
60 ml /4 tbls freshly grated Parmesan cheese
salt
freshly ground black pepper
60 ml /4 tbls olive oil
50 g /2 oz butter
1 Spanish onion, coarsely chopped
4 tomatoes, skinned, seeded and chopped

1 Poach the courgettes in boiling water until just tender, 5–8 minutes. Drain thoroughly, allow them to cool and slice thickly. Dry each slice on absorbent paper.
2 Combine the flour with the freshly grated Parmesan cheese and salt and freshly ground black pepper to taste. Toss the courgette slices in this mixture until they are lightly coated.
3 Heat the oil in a heavy frying pan and sauté the courgettes over a moderate heat until they are golden brown on all sides. Remove from the pan with a slotted spoon. Drain thoroughly on absorbent paper and keep hot.
4 Melt the butter in the pan and sauté the coarsely chopped onion until it is soft and transparent. Add the chopped tomatoes and simmer for 2–3 minutes longer.
5 Pile the courgettes in the centre of a heated serving dish and surround them with the sautéed onion and tomato mixture.

20 minutes

Fruit medley

Serves 4
1 ripe pear, peeled and cored
2 peaches
juice of 1 orange
¼ pineapple
50 g /2 oz grapes or 2 kiwi fruit
100 g /4 oz raspberries or strawberries
100 g /4 oz red plums or red cherries
50 g /2 oz vanilla sugar (see note below)
125 ml /4 fl oz passion fruit juice or other sweet fruit juice
½ kiwi fruit, sliced, to garnish
whipped cream, to serve

1 Cut the pear into chunks. Skin and stone the peaches and chop the flesh into chunks. Put the fruit in a large shallow dish, pour in the orange juice and toss the fruit.
2 Peel the pineapple, slice it, then cut into chunks, removing the core. Seed the grapes, or peel the kiwi fruit, and cut into chunks. Hull the strawberries, if using.
3 Stone and halve the plums or stone the cherries. Add half the raspberries or strawberries and the remaining fruit, plus any fruit juices, to the dish. Gently spoon the orange juice over the fruit. Sprinkle with the vanilla sugar and macerate for 1–2 hours.
4 Purée the reserved strawberries or raspberries through a sieve. Divide the purée among 4 glass dishes, then divide the fruit and their juices among the dishes.
5 About 1 hour before serving, pour on the passion or other sweet fruit juice. Chill the fruit salad, then garnish with kiwi fruit and serve with whipped cream.

● This fruit salad is based on an Imperial Russian recipe where the fruit juice is replaced by very sweet champagne or another sweet sparkling wine.
● A vanilla pod buried in a jar of caster sugar for at least two weeks will impregnate the sugar with a delicate vanilla flavour.

 35 minutes, plus chilling

Chocolate banana pie

Serves 4–6
15 ml /1 tbls cornflour
150 g /5 oz caster sugar
300 ml /10 fl oz milk
3 eggs, separated
2.5 ml /½ tsp vanilla essence
125 g /4 oz plain chocolate, roughly grated
2 bananas
23 cm /9 in fully baked pastry case made with 175 g /6 oz flour
15 ml /1 tbls finely grated orange zest
15 g /½ oz gelatine, dissolved in 15 ml /1 tbls water
For the decoration
75 g /3 oz plain chocolate, roughly grated
½ banana
5 ml /1 tsp lemon juice

1 In a saucepan, mix the cornflour and 75 g /3 oz of the sugar together. Bring the milk almost to boiling point.
2 In a bowl, beat the egg yolks until pale, then slowly pour the hot milk onto them. Pour the egg and milk mixture onto the cornflour mixture. Cook it very slowly, stirring constantly, over a low heat until the custard thickens and coats the back of a spoon. Remove it from the heat and add the vanilla essence.
3 Pour half the custard into a bowl and add the grated chocolate. Stir until the chocolate has melted. Slice the bananas and arrange them in the bottom of the pastry case. Pour in the chocolate custard. Cool, then chill.
4 Add the grated orange zest and dissolved gelatine to the other half of the custard and mix well. Chill for 30 minutes or until it is slightly thick.
5 Beat the egg whites until frothy. Add the remaining sugar, beat it well, then fold into the chilled custard mixture. Pour it over the chocolate custard layer. Return to the refrigerator until set.
6 To serve, remove the pie from the refrigerator 15 minutes before you need it. Decorate the pie with the grated chocolate. Cut the half banana into 5 pieces, arrange on top of the pie and brush each piece with lemon juice.

● Try adding 30 ml /2 tbls Grand Marnier to this recipe to enhance the orange flavour.

 2½ hours, including chilling

Entertaining
Friends

A TASTE OF THE EXOTIC

*Japanese beef with
fresh ginger*

*Guinea fowl
with fresh fruits*

Rice with pine nuts

*Vanilla-poached pears
with raspberry sauce*

Wine: *Rheingau*

Planning menus for friends rather than the family means a chance to experiment with more unconventional dishes without the risk of some small voice being raised in alarm! Foreign, exotic dishes must come top of the list for those who want to be more adventurous. One good choice for entertaining is a meal *à la nouvelle cuisine*. This is a style of cooking which not only provides guests with a topic of conversation because of its attractive Oriental presentation but which is characterized by relatively quick and easy-to-prepare recipes.

Simplicity is the keyword. Among others, *nouvelle cuisine* relies on three principles to achieve its effect: the use of absolutely fresh vegetables, fruit and other produce; fast last-minute cooking, often with no advance preparation; and the traditional presentation and garnishes of the ancient Chinese, Thai or Japanese kitchen. The natural flavours of the food predominate and care is taken not to smother them with over-strong seasoning or rich sauces. If sauces are used, they tend to be light and made not with butter and flour but by reducing meat juices, wines, meat or vegetable stocks.

I have chosen a *nouvelle cuisine* meal for my first set menu in this section. Japanese beef with fresh ginger is the starter: this is a combination of rare beef eaten with a sweet and sour marinade. The simple, geometric Japanese garnish is typical of Eastern presentation and lends an attractive finishing touch. Guinea fowl served with fresh fruits for the main course combines the fresh flavours of passion fruit, pawpaw, kiwi fruit and strawberries with this delicate tasting bird. Arrange the slices of fruit around the meat and serve accompanied by Rice with pine nuts. Chilled Vanilla-poached pears with raspberry sauce provides a sweet and colourful end to the meal.

Plan-ahead timetable

On the day before the meal
Vanilla-poached pears: make the dessert.
Japanese beef with ginger: make the marinade.

Three hours before the meal
Guinea fowl with fresh fruits: remove the guinea fowl from the refrigerator. Make the stuffing.
Japanese beef with ginger: blanch and refresh the strips of carrot and chive. Brush the beef with oil and fold up.

One hour before the meal

Guinea fowl with fresh fruits: stuff the guinea fowl. Season, spread with butter and roast. Reduce the meat glaze, dry white wine and Madeira. Add the passion fruit juice and season. Remove from the heat.

Fifteen minutes before the meal

Japanese beef with ginger: arrange the beef on individual plates with the marinade. Garnish.
Guinea fowl with fresh fruits: remove the guinea fowl from the oven, discard stuffing. Cut into portions and keep hot.

Just before the meal

Rice with pine nuts: cook the rice.

Between the first and the main course

Guinea fowl with fresh fruits: bring the sauce back to the boil, remove from the heat, whisk in the butter. Pour over the guinea fowl, garnish and serve.
Rice with pine nuts: sauté the nuts, mix with rice and serve.

Between the main course and the dessert

Vanilla-poached pears: pour over the sauce, and decorate.

Japanese beef with fresh ginger

Serves 4
32 julienne strips of carrot
32 × 5 cm /2 in lengths of chive
16 long, thin slices rare sirloin, about 20 × 5 cm /8 × 2 in
45–60 ml /3–4 tbls sesame seed oil
For the marinade
1 ginger root
juice of 1 lime
60 ml /4 tbls clear honey
20 ml /4 tsp soy sauce

1 To make the marinade, peel the ginger root and cut into julienne strips. In a small bowl, combine the lime juice, the honey and soy sauce. Add the julienne strips of ginger and leave to marinate for at least 2 hours.
2 Blanch the julienne strips of carrot in simmering water for 2–3 minutes, drain and refresh. Blanch the lengths of chive, drain and refresh.
3 Brush the strips of beef with the sesame seed oil. Lay 1 strip of beef with the short edge towards you, fold it into 3 from the short edge, to make a neat, rectangular package. Repeat with the remaining strips of beef.
4 To serve, place 4 pieces of beef on each individual plate. Accompany the beef with the marinade in a small Chinese-style bowl on the plate or remove the julienne strips of ginger from the marinade with a slotted spoon and place some in the centre of each individual plate. Moisten with a little of the marinade if wished. Garnish the beef squares with 2 julienne strips of carrot and 2 lengths of chive, crossed diagonally.

● Use left-over beef for this starter or buy slices or rare sirloin from a delicatessen.

 2 hours marinating, then 15 minutes

Guinea fowl with fresh fruits

Serves 4
900 g /2 lb (dressed weight)
  guinea fowl
salt
freshly ground black pepper
15 g /½ oz butter, softened
15 ml /1 tbls meat glaze
  (see page 16)
60 ml /4 tbls dry white wine
60 ml /4 tbls Madeira
50 g /2 oz cold butter, diced

For the stuffing
4 passion fruit
60 ml /4 tbls fresh breadcrumbs
1 medium onion, chopped
15 g /½ oz butter, softened
15 ml /1 tbls chopped fresh parsley
salt and ground black pepper
For the garnish
1 kiwi fruit, sliced
4 strawberries, sliced
1 pawpaw, sliced

1 Remove the guinea fowl from the refrigerator and bring it to room temperature. Heat the oven to 180C /350F /gas 4. Trim any feathers or quills from the guinea fowl and wipe it with a damp cloth.
2 Make the stuffing. Cut the passion fruit in half, scoop out the pulp and press it through a sieve. Reserve the juice for the sauce.
3 Mix the fruit pulp with the breadcrumbs, onion, butter and parsley and season with salt and freshly ground black pepper to taste. Stuff the guinea fowl, sew up the vent and truss. Season the bird with salt and freshly ground black pepper and spread the breast with the softened butter. Roast the bird in the oven for 45 minutes, or until it is tender.
4 Meanwhile, in a small pan, bring the meat glaze, dry white wine and Madeira to the boil. Boil until they are reduced to half their original quantity. Add the passion fruit juice and season the sauce with salt and freshly ground black pepper to taste.
5 Remove the guinea fowl from the oven and undo the trussing and thread. Discard the stuffing. Cut the guinea fowl into 4 or 8 serving pieces. Place on a heated serving dish and keep warm.
6 To finish the sauce, bring it back to the boil, then remove it from the heat and whisk in the cold diced butter, a little at a time.
7 Pour the sauce over the guinea fowl portions and garnish with the sliced kiwi fruit, strawberries and papaw. Serve immediately.

● Store your surplus meat glaze in a jar in the refrigerator; or freeze it in an ice-cube tray for use in another sauce.
● To prepare the pawpaw, cut it open like a melon and then scoop out the mass of black seeds. Peel and shape the slices.
● When pawpaws are not available, use melon instead.

 1¼ hours   Rheingau

Rice with pine nuts

Serves 4
250 g /8 oz long-grain rice
salt
25 g /1 oz butter
25 g /1 oz pine nuts
freshly ground black pepper
For the garnish
lime slices
flat-leaved parsley

1 Bring 425 ml /15 fl oz salted water to the boil. Dribble the rice gradually into the pan, cover and boil gently for 15–18 minutes, or until all the liquid has been absorbed and the rice is tender.
2 Meanwhile, melt the butter in a frying-pan and sauté the pine nuts until they are golden brown. Mix the pine nuts into the rice with a fork and season with salt and freshly ground black pepper. Transfer to a heated serving dish and serve immediately, garnished with lime slices and flat-leaved parsley.

● Pine nuts are used in many Middle Eastern and Mediterranean recipes. They are sometimes known as pine kernels or pignolias and are the seeds of certain varieties of pine tree. Their shells are impossible to crack by hand so they are always sold shelled. The texture of the nut is distinctively soft and slightly oily. They are expensive to buy so, if you wish, blanched almonds can be used as a substitute, although the taste is different.

 20 minutes

Vanilla-poached pears with raspberry sauce

Serves 4
4 medium-sized pears
juice of ½ lemon
250 g /8 oz sugar
½ cinnamon stick
1 clove
1 thin strip of orange zest
1 thin strip of lemon zest
5 ml /1 tsp vanilla essence
150 ml /5 fl oz dry white wine
red food colouring (optional)
crystallized violets or toasted almonds, to garnish
For the raspberry sauce
275 g /10 oz fresh or frozen raspberries
15 ml /1 tbls icing sugar
lemon juice

1 Peel the pears but do not core them. As they are peeled, drop them into a bowl of cold water acidulated with lemon juice, to prevent them from turning brown.
2 Pour 275 ml /10 fl oz water into a pan large enough to hold the pears upright side by side. Add the sugar, spices, strips of zest and the vanilla essence. Bring to the boil, stirring with a wooden spoon until the sugar has dissolved. Add the pears. Cover the pan and simmer for about 15 minutes, shaking the pan from time to time.
3 Pour in the white wine and continue to cook over a low heat, uncovered, for 15–30 minutes, or until the pears are meltingly tender but not mushy.
4 With a slotted spoon, transfer the pears to a deep serving dish. Boil the cooking juices rapidly until they have reduced to the consistency of a light syrup, then, if desired, colour pale pink with a drop or two of red food colouring. Spoon the syrup over the pears, to glaze them. Allow to cool. Chill.
5 To make the raspberry sauce, defrost the frozen raspberries, if using. Rub the fruit through a fine sieve, or purée the raspberries in a blender and sieve to remove the seeds. Add the icing sugar and lemon juice to taste. Chill.
6 To serve the pears, spoon a little raspberry sauce over the pears and sprinkle with crystallized violets or toasted almonds.

1½ hours,
plus chilling

SOMETHING SOPHISTICATED

Plaice fillets with cheddar soufflé

~

Tournedos Henri IV

Bearnaise sauce
Green beans with mushrooms
New potatoes with chive butter

~

Strawberry meringue chantilly

Wine: Côtes de Ventoux

Plaice fillets with Cheddar soufflé

Serves 6

butter, for greasing
6 plaice fillets (about 75 g /3 oz each)
salt and freshly ground black pepper
150 ml /5 fl oz fish stock or water
6 slices of tomato
65 ml /2½ fl oz mayonnaise
2 eggs, separated
100 g /4 oz Cheddar cheese, finely grated
75 ml /3 fl oz thick cream

1 Heat the oven to 220C /425F /gas 7. Butter the base of a heavy-based saucepan and 6 ramekin dishes, 150 ml /5 fl oz capacity each.
2 Trim and skin the plaice fillets and sprinkle them with salt and freshly ground black pepper. Roll up each fillet from the narrowest end and secure the roll with a cocktail stick. Plaice the rolled fillets in the buttered saucepan and cover with the fish stock or water. Stand the pan over a medium heat until the liquid is barely simmering, then reduce the heat and poach the fish gently for 2–3 minutes. Remove the fillets from the pan with a slotted spoon and drain them well on absorbent paper. Remove the cocktail sticks.
3 Cut each tomato slice into 4, to make them easy to eat, then re-assemble each slice in a buttered ramekin dish. Place a fish fillet on top of each tomato slice.
4 Place the mayonnaise in a medium-sized bowl with the egg yolks and grated cheese. Mix well, and season to taste with salt and freshly ground black pepper.
5 Whisk the egg whites until stiff. Whip the cream until it stands in soft peaks. Using a large metal spoon, fold the cream into the cheese mixture, then gently fold in the egg white. Divide the mixture among the ramekin dishes.
6 Place the dishes on a baking tray and bake in the oven for 15 minutes, until risen and golden brown. Serve immediately.

45 minutes

Tournedos Henri IV

Serves 6

6 tournedos — round fillet steaks, cut about 3 cm /1¼ in thick
*   and encased in a thin band of fat tied with string*
freshly ground black pepper
olive oil
6 large thick slices white bread
40 g /1½ oz butter
6 perfect button mushroom caps, cut as minarets (see picture)
salt
6 large fresh watercress sprigs, to garnish
Bearnaise sauce, to serve (see recipe)

1 Sprinkle the steaks on both sides with freshly ground black pepper. Now sprinkle them lightly with olive oil.
2 Heat the grill at the maximum temperature.
3 Trim the bread slices into neat rounds slightly larger than the steaks. Heat 60 ml /4 tbls olive oil and 25 g /1 oz butter in a frying-pan, and, when hot, sauté the bread slices gently until crisp and golden on both sides. Drain on absorbent paper and keep hot. Sauté the mushroom caps in 15 g /½ oz butter until just tender. Keep hot.
4 Grill the steaks, with the grill rack 7.5–10 cm /3–4 in from the source of the heat, for about 8 minutes on each side, if you like them rare, longer if you prefer them medium-rare or well done. Season to taste with salt. Cut the strings and remove the fat.
5 Arrange the sautéed bread rounds on a heated serving dish. Lay a tournedo on each round and top each with a sautéed button mushroom cap. Garnish the serving dish with sprigs of fresh watercress and serve immediately. Accompany with the bearnaise sauce passed round separately in a sauceboat.

● Henry IV, the best loved of French kings, was born in Pau, the capital of Bearn, and he was called the *Great Bearnaise*. Bearnaise sauce, an egg and lemon sauce, almost like a warm mayonnaise, was named to honour him in the 19th century.

40 minutes

Côtes de Ventoux or
another red Côtes du Rhône

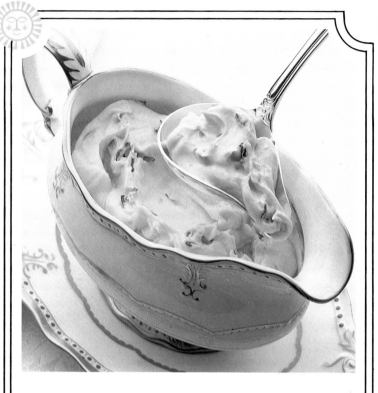

Bearnaise sauce

Serves 6

4–6 tarragon sprigs, coarsely chopped
4–6 chervil sprigs, coarsely chopped
15 ml /1 tbls chopped shallot
2 black peppercorns, crushed
30 ml /2 tbls tarragon vinegar
150 ml /5 fl oz dry white wine
3 egg yolks
225 g /8 oz butter, diced, then softened
salt
lemon juice
a pinch of cayenne pepper

1 In a saucepan, combine half the coarsely chopped herbs with the chopped shallot, crushed black peppercorns, tarragon vinegar and white wine. Bring to the boil and cook over a high heat until the liquid is reduced to about 30 ml /2 tbls in the bottom of the pan. Remove from the heat.
2 Beat the egg yolks with 15 ml /1 tbls water and put them in the top pan of a double boiler with the reduced liquid. Put the pan onto the boiler containing hot, but not boiling, water. Stir briskly with a wire whisk until light and fluffy.
3 Add some of the butter, a piece at a time, to the egg mixture, whisking briskly until completely incorporated. As the sauce begins to thicken, add a little more butter, whisking thoroughly until it is incorporated. Add more butter, whisking it in thoroughly as before, until the sauce is thick and all the butter is used.
4 Season to taste with salt, lemon juice and cayenne pepper.
5 Strain the sauce through a fine sieve to remove any threads of egg white and to give it a fine gloss. Stir in the remaining chopped herbs and serve warm.

● Like its near cousin, hollandaise sauce, the secret of a successful bearnaise is never to let the water in the bottom pan of the double boiler reach boiling point, or the sauce will not 'take'.
● Bearnaise sauce is the perfect accompaniment to grilled steak; try it, too, with grilled, poached or fried fish.
● Bearnaise sauce is always served warm. If you make it ahead it can be kept in a wide-necked Thermos, but is better kept warm, covered, on top of the double boiler.

🔪 25 minutes

Green beans with mushrooms

Serves 6

500 g /1 lb frozen French beans, halved
50 g /2 oz butter
30 ml /2 tbls olive oil
60 ml /4 tbls onion, finely chopped
225 g /8 oz large button mushrooms, thinly sliced
lemon juice
salt and freshly ground black pepper
30 ml /2 tbls finely chopped fresh parsley

1 Boil the beans until tender but still crisp. Drain and refresh under cold running water. Melt the butter with the olive oil in a large saucepan. Sauté the finely chopped onion until it becomes transparent.
2 Add the thinly sliced mushrooms and sauté them until they are tender.
3 Add the cooked and halved green beans and toss for a few minutes, or until the beans are warmed through.
4 Sprinkle with lemon juice and salt and freshly ground black pepper to taste. Toss once more to blend the flavours.
5 To serve, transfer the beans and mushrooms to a heated dish. Sprinkle with the finely chopped fresh parsley and serve immediately.

🔪 1 hour

New potatoes with chive butter

Serves 6
1 kg /2 lb new potatoes, scrubbed
2.5 ml /½ tsp coarse salt
50 g /2 oz butter
60 ml /4 tbls snipped chives

1 Place the potatoes in a large saucepan and pour in enough boiling water to cover. Add the salt and set the pan over high heat. Bring the water to the boil again; reduce the heat to low and simmer the potatoes for 20–25 minutes or until they are tender.
2 Remove the pan from the heat and drain the potatoes in a colander. Carefully peel the skins off the potatoes, holding them in a cloth, so you do not burn your hands. Transfer the potatoes to a warmed serving dish and keep warm.
3 In a small saucepan, melt the butter over a moderate heat. When the foam subsides, remove the pan from the heat and stir in the snipped chives.
4 Spoon the hot chive-flavoured butter over the potatoes and toss, to coat them thoroughly. Serve immediately.

15 minutes

Strawberry meringue chantilly

Serves 6–8
5 egg whites
275 g /10 oz caster sugar
500 g /1 lb fresh strawberries, hulled, cleaned and chilled
For the crème chantilly
275–425 ml /10–15 fl oz thick cream

15–30 ml /1–2 tbls icing sugar, sieved
15–30 ml /1–2 tbls iced water
For the fresh strawberry sauce
500 g /1 lb strawberries
30 ml /2 tbls icing sugar, sieved
15–30 ml /1–2 tbls lemon juice

1 Heat the oven to 150C /300F /gas 2. Using a plate as a guide, draw a 23 cm /9 in circle on a sheet of non-stick silicone paper. Place the paper on a baking sheet.
2 Whisk the egg whites in a large mixing bowl until they form stiff peaks when the beater is removed. Whisk in 50 g /2 oz of the sugar and continue whisking for 1 minute or until the mixture is very stiff and glossy. Using a metal spoon, fold in remaining sugar.
3 Spread one third of the mixture onto the circle of paper to make a layer about 6 mm /¼ in thick. Fill a large piping bag, fitted with a 25 mm /1 in star nozzle, with the remaining mixture and pipe the mixture around the edge of the circle in decorative swirls so as to form a case.
4 Bake the meringue for 1 hour. Turn off the oven and leave the meringue in the oven for a further 10–15 minutes, or until it is crisp on the outside but still soft in the centre.
5 Meanwhile make the crème chantilly. Whisk the thick cream until soft peaks form. Add the sieved icing sugar, to taste, and beat until stiff. Add the iced water and fold it in until the cream is smooth. Chill it in the refrigerator.
6 To make the fresh strawberry sauce, rinse the strawberries only if necessary, drain and purée in a blender. Pass the purée through a fine sieve to make it quite smooth. Add the sieved icing sugar and lemon juice to taste, mixing well. Chill until needed.
7 Remove the baking sheet from the oven and leave the meringue to cool completely. When cold, lift it off the baking sheet and carefully remove and discard the paper from bottom of the meringue. Set aside.
8 Place the meringue case on a decorative serving plate and spoon the créme chantilly into it. Pile the prepared strawberries onto the top of the cream and serve with the strawberry sauce, in a jug.

1½ hours, plus cooling

FOR A SPECIAL OCCASION

Mousse of smoked mackerel

Lamb in Greek pastry

Glazed courgettes

Carrots poulettes

Chocolate gateau

Wine: Castel Danielis

Plan-ahead timetable

On the morning of the meal
Mousse of smoked mackerel: prepare the mousse and chill.
Lamb in Greek pastry: make the tomato roses for the garnish; stone the olives.

Early in the afternoon
Chocolate gateau: prepare the sponge, bake and cool.
Prepare the fillings. Assemble the cake, cover with cream and store in a cool place.
Lamb in Greek pastry: prepare the mushroom duxelles, and brown the cutlets. Leave to cool.

One and a half hours before the meal
Lamb in Greek pastry: fold the filo (or roll out the puff pastry). Make the parcels and glaze.
Carrots poulettes: cook the carrots. Reserve. Make the sauce.

Twenty minutes before the meal
Lamb in Greek pastry: put in the oven to cook.
Mousse of smoked mackerel: spoon the mousse into individual ramekins and garnish. Toast the bread.
Glazed courgettes: prepare and cook the courgettes.

Just before the main course
Carrots poulettes: add the carrots to the sauce and reheat.
Lamb in Greek pastry: garnish and put on cutlet frills.

Mousse of smoked mackerel

Serves 6
500 g /1 lb smoked mackerel fillets
90–120 ml /6–8 tbls thick cream
90 ml /6 tbls olive oil
30–45 ml /2–3 tbls lemon juice
salt and freshly ground black pepper
To garnish
6 lemon twists
6 tiny sprigs of fresh parsley
To serve
fingers of hot toast
chilled butter

1 Skin the mackerel fillets and remove any bones. Place them in a blender and purée them into a paste.
2 Gradually and separately add 30 ml /2 tbls each of thick cream, olive oil and lemon juice to the blender goblet and whisk in. Each addition should be beaten in before the next is added, as in making mayonnaise. Now beat in the remaining thick cream, olive oil and lemon juice to taste, a little at a time, until the mousse is smooth.
3 Season the mousse with salt and freshly ground black pepper to taste. Chill in the refrigerator until ready to serve. If the mousse seems too firm when you remove it from the refrigerator, beat in a little more cream, olive oil or lemon juice, or a combination of all three of these.
4 Before serving, spoon the mousse into 6 small ramekins. Garnish each one with a twist of lemon and a tiny sprig of parsley. Serve with fingers of hot toast and chilled butter.

● The quality of the smoked fish will make a great deal of difference to the amount of oil and cream the mixture can absorb. Packaged mackerel fillets tend to absorb more than freshly smoked mackerel.

 30 minutes,
plus chilling

Lamb in Greek pastry

Serves 6
6 lamb cutlets, trimmed of fat
salt and ground black pepper
15 g /½ oz butter
15 ml /1 tbls olive oil
6 sheets (about 150 g /5 oz) filo
pastry, or 200 g /7 oz puff
pastry, defrosted
50 g /2 oz melted butter (if using
filo pastry)
75 g /3 oz pâté de foie, cut into
6 small rounds
beaten egg

For the duxelles
15 g /½ oz butter
½ Spanish onion, finely chopped
50 g /2 oz mushrooms, finely
chopped
50 g /2 oz cooked ham, finely
chopped
salt and freshly ground black
pepper
For the garnish
6 tomato roses (see recipe)
sprigs of flat-leaved fresh parsley
6 black olives, stoned

1 Season the lamb cutlets with salt and freshly ground black pepper.
In a pan, heat the butter and olive oil and brown the cutlets for 2–3
minutes on each side. Remove them from the pan and then allow
them to cool.
2 Meanwhile, to prepare the mushroom duxelles, melt the butter in
a pan and sauté the onion until it is transparent. Add the mushrooms
and continue to sauté gently until soft. Stir in the ham; season with
salt and freshly ground black pepper to taste and remove from the
heat. Let the mixture cool. Heat the oven to 220C /425F /gas 7.
3 If using filo pastry, take one sheet at a time and fold it in half to
make a rectangle. Brush lightly all over with melted butter. Place a
round of pâté de foie in the centre of the pastry, then cover this with
15 ml /1 tbls of the mushroom duxelles. Lay a lamb cutlet on top of
this, arranging it so that the meat 'eye' of the cutlet covers the
duxelles. Fold the nearside edge of the pastry over the cutlet and the
two short sides in towards the centre. Brush the folds with melted
butter. Fold over the other long side and twist the pastry around the
cutlet bone neatly to seal it completely. Lay on a baking sheet, seam
side down, and brush all over with melted butter.
4 If using puff pastry, divide it into 6 equal pieces. Roll each piece
out very thinly into a rectangle about 20 × 12 cm /8 × 5 in. Proceed as
in step 3, using beaten egg to seal the edges and trimming off excess
pastry as you go. Lay the parcels on a baking sheet, seam side down,
and brush the tops with beaten egg to glaze them.
5 Bake the parcels for 30–35 minutes, or until well puffed and
golden brown. Decorate with cutlet frills. Serve garnished with the
tomato roses (made by thinly paring away the skin of a tomato and
coiling it around your little finger), parsley and black olives.

 1½ hours   Castel Danielis

Glazed courgettes

Serves 6
750 g /1½ lb courgettes
salt
90 ml /6 tbls chicken stock, home-made or from a cube
40 g /1½ oz butter
freshly ground black pepper
For the garnish
onion rings
sprigs of flat-leaved parsley

1 Wipe the courgettes with a damp cloth and slice off the ends. Cut
each one into four lengthways. Cut each piece in half.
2 Bring a saucepan of salted water to the boil. Add the pieces of
courgette and simmer for 3 minutes. Drain and keep warm.
3 In a clean saucepan, combine the chicken stock and the butter.
Bring to the boil and add the drained courgettes. Season with salt and
freshly ground black pepper. Simmer for 5–7 minutes or until the
courgettes are tender and the liquid reduced to a syrupy glaze. Stir
with a wooden spoon from time to time.
4 Transfer the glazed courgettes to a heated serving dish. Serve
immediately, garnished with onion rings and flat-leaved parsley.

15 minutes

Carrots poulettes

Serves 6
1 kg /2 lb small, whole carrots
salt
25 g /1 oz butter
30 ml /2 tbls flour
⅓ chicken stock cube, crumbled
juice of ½ lemon
30 ml /2 tbls thick cream
1 egg yolk
white pepper
15 ml /1 tbls finely chopped fresh parsley

1 Scrape the carrots and cook them in boiling salted water for 10–15 minutes, or until tender. Drain the carrots, reserving the cooking liquid.
2 Melt the butter in a saucepan, stir in the flour to make a roux and cook for 2–3 minutes. Gradually stir in 275 ml /10 fl oz of the reserved carrot cooking liquid and add the crumbled chicken stock cube. Bring the sauce to the boil over a low heat, then simmer for about 10 minutes.
3 Meanwhile, in a bowl combine the lemon juice, thick cream, 30 ml /2 tbls of the hot sauce and the egg yolk and mix well. Stir the egg yolk mixture into the sauce and cook it, stirring, over a low heat until it thickens — do not allow the sauce to boil or the egg and cream will curdle. Season with salt and white pepper to taste. Add the carrots to the sauce and heat through. Pour into a heated serving dish, garnish with finely chopped parsley and serve immediately.

● This recipe shows you how easy it is in practice to make classic velouté sauce for vegetables. The vegetable water and the stock cube supply the stock base. A roux is used to thicken the sauce and then it is finished off with a liaison of cream and egg yolks. This sauce takes its name from a young hen, a *poulette*, because originally it was associated with a poached chicken dish.

 45 minutes

Chocolate gateau

Serves 6
melted butter and flour, for the cake tin
75 g /3 oz flour
15 g /½ oz cocoa powder
15 g /½ oz cornflour
3 eggs
75 g /3 oz caster sugar
50 g /2 oz butter, melted
For the chocolate filling
3 eggs, separated
25 g /1 oz caster sugar
175 g /6 oz bitter chocolate
25 g /1 oz butter
15 ml /1 tbls grated orange zest
salt
To assemble the cake
30 ml /2 tbls Cointreau
275 ml /10 fl oz thick cream, whipped
15 ml /1 tbls grated orange zest
50 g /2 oz chocolate vermicelli

1 Heat the oven to 180C /350F /gas 4. Brush a loose-bottomed 20 cm / 8 in cake tin with melted butter. Line the base with greaseproof paper and brush with more butter. Lightly coat the tin with flour.
2 Make the chocolate genoise sponge; sift the flour, cocoa powder and cornflour together 3 times.
3 In another bowl, combine the eggs and sugar. Set the bowl over a pan of simmering water and whisk until thick, light and lukewarm (about 10 minutes).
4 Remove the bowl from the heat and continue whisking until the mixture has cooled and leaves a trail when the beaters are lifted. Resift the flour mixture over the surface. Fold in with a metal spoon.
5 Cool the melted butter and fold it in quickly. Pour the mixture into the tin. Bake in the oven for 25–30 minutes. When cooked, turn onto a wire rack. Peel off the lining paper and leave to cool.
6 Meanwhile, make the chocolate filling; in a bowl beat the egg yolks with the caster sugar until creamy and lemon-coloured.
7 Melt the chocolate with the butter in a bowl over hot water.
8 Add the melted chocolate and finely grated orange zest to the beaten egg yolk mixture. The next step must be done quickly or the chocolate will set too hard to work.
9 Add a pinch of salt to the egg whites and whisk until stiff but not dry. Fold the egg whites into the chocolate mixture. Spoon the mixture into a 600 ml /1 pt dish, chill and set.
10 Cut the cake into two layers. Sprinkle the insides of the layers with Cointreau and spread the bottom layer with the chilled chocolate filling. Replace the top layer. Fold the grated orange zest into the cream. Cover the cake sides with a thin layer, leaving enough cream mixture to cover and decorate the top. Coat the sides of the cake with chocolate vermicelli. Cover the top of the cake with cream and pipe a cream border around the outer edge.

 3 hours, including chilling

A GOURMET MENU

Turbot en brochettes

Veal with cucumbers and mange tout
Sauté potatoes
Orange and chicory salad

Choux cream puffs

Cheeseboard

Wine: Chablis

A meal may be memorable for the food or for the company — most of us hope that our parties offer both good food and a comfortable atmosphere. You choose your guests to complement each other, combining personalities and interests. In the same way, choose your menu carefully, balancing one dish against another for blends and contrasts of colour, texture and flavour. The care with which you present each dish should make your guests feel truly cosseted.

Try starting with a quick and easy skewer dish. Turbot en brochettes, with peppers and tomatoes, make a simple and elegant appetizer. They are especially good accompanied with simple, tangy Lemon butter.

Follow this appetizing starter with a creamy dish of Veal with cucumbers and mange tout. Braised in a sauce made from white wine and chicken stock with tiny button onions, the veal is served with crunchy cucumber pieces and mange tout, cooked for a few minutes on top of the meat. The sauce is smoothly finished with thick cream. With it I suggest you serve Sauté potatoes.

After the rich main course, your guests will like to refresh their palates with Orange and chicory salad. Don't hurry them at this stage: let them savour and relax before continuing to the dessert, which is a treasure in the shape of Choux cream puffs. You can save time with this dessert by making the choux pastry cases the day before the meal. Then, shortly before you eat, fill them with creamy Crème St Honoré, sprinkle them with icing sugar and decorate with perfect red strawberries. End the meal by offering your guests a selection of ripe cheeses served with fresh grapes, dates or apples.

Plan-ahead timetable

On the day before the meal
Veal with cucumbers and mange tout: make the chicken stock unless you are using a stock cube.
Choux cream puffs: make the choux pastry and pipe it onto a greased baking sheet. Cook and then cool on a wire rack, then store overnight in an airtight tin.

Three and a half hours before the meal
Veal with cucumbers and mange tout: cut the meat and bring it to room temperature. Prepare the vegetables.
Choux cream puffs: make and cool the Crème St Honoré, then fill the puffs and put them in the refrigerator.

Two and a half hours before the meal

Turbot en brochettes: cut the turbot, green peppers and tomatoes into bite-sized pieces; marinate and then thread them onto the skewers. Prepare the lemon butter.

Orange and chicory salad: wash and slice the oranges, chicory and lettuce following the recipe. Arrange on individual plates or in a bowl. Make the dressing.

One hour forty minutes before the meal

Veal with cucumbers and mange tout: sauté and reserve the veal and onions. Reduce the wine. Return the veal to the pan, cover and cook.

Cheeseboard: take the cheeses from the refrigerator and arrange them on the board.

Thirty minutes before the meal

Choux cream puffs: decorate with icing sugar and strawberries and reserve in the refrigerator.

Sauté potatoes: wash and chop the potatoes and then fry them. Keep them hot in the oven until needed.

Veal with cucumbers and mange toute: add the sautéed onions.

Ten minutes before the meal

Turbot en brochettes: grill, then serve with lemon butter.

Between the main course and the dessert

Choux cream puffs: remove the puffs from the refrigerator.

Orange and chicory salad: spoon the dressing over the salad and then serve.

Turbot en brochettes

Serves 4–6
1.4 kg /3 lb turbot
200 ml /7 fl oz olive oil, plus extra for greasing
7.5 ml /1½ tsp chopped fresh thyme
7.5 ml /1½ tsp chopped rosemary
7.5 ml /1½ tsp fennel, chopped
salt and freshly ground black pepper
3 green or red peppers
6 tomatoes, quartered and seeded
For the lemon butter
175 g /6 oz butter, softened
juice of 1 large lemon
cayenne pepper

1 Remove the skin and bones from the turbot. Cut the flesh into 25 mm /1 in cubes.
2 In a bowl, combine the olive oil and the freshly chopped thyme, rosemary and fennel. Season with salt and freshly ground black pepper.
3 Halve, core and seed the peppers. Cut each pepper into 8 squares. Add the turbot cubes and the tomatoes. Toss to coat with the marinade and leave for 10 minutes.
4 Heat the grill to high.
5 Meanwhile, prepare the lemon butter. In a bowl, cream the softened butter until it is almost runny. Beat in the lemon juice, a little at a time, and season with cayenne pepper to taste. Transfer to a sauce-boat.
6 Grease 4–6 20 cm /8 in skewers. Thread a piece of tomato followed by a cube of turbot and then a piece of pepper onto the skewers. Continue until all the ingredients are used up.
7 Brush the grid of the grill pan with a little olive oil. Lay the tubot brochettes side by side on the grid and grill 7.5 cm /3 in from the heat for 6 minutes, turning the brochettes once during cooking and basting with the marinade.
8 Transfer to a heated serving platter and serve immediately with the lemon butter.

 1 hour

Veal with cucumbers and mange tout

Serves 4
1.1 kg /2 ½ lb pie veal
freshly ground black pepper
salt
30 ml /2 tbls olive oil
25 g /1 oz butter
225 g /8 oz tiny button onions, peeled
275 ml /10 fl oz dry white wine
150 ml /5 fl oz chicken stock, home-made or from a cube
bouquet garni
1½ cucumbers, peeled, seeded and cut into 20 mm /¾ in dice
225 g /8 oz mange tout, trimmed
90 ml /6 tbls thick cream
snipped fresh chives, to garnish

1 Cut the veal into 5 cm /2 in pieces, discarding any fat and gristle. Season generously with freshly ground black pepper and leave to come to room temperature. Just before cooking, season to taste with salt.
2 Heat the olive oil and the butter in a heavy casserole. When the foaming subsides, add enough veal pieces to cover the bottom of the pan and sauté for 2 minutes each side, or until golden brown. Remove with a slotted spoon and repeat with the remaining veal.
3 Add the onions to the pan and sauté for 3 minutes, or until lightly golden, shaking the pan occasionally. Remove with a slotted spoon and reserve.
4 Discard any fats remaining in the pan. Pour in the wine and bring to the boil, scraping the pan to remove any sediment. Boil rapidly, until the wine has reduced to half its original quantity.
5 Pour in the stock and bring to simmering point. Return the sautéed veal to the pan with the bouquet garni. Adjust the seasoning and cover with a tight-fitting lid. Alternatively, use a sheet of foil, then the lid. Simmer gently for 1 hour.
6 Add the reserved onions and stir to mix. Cover and cook for a further 15 minutes, or until the veal is tender. Add the cucumbers and mange tout, cover and cook for a further 5 minutes, or until the mange tout are cooked but still crisp.
7 With a slotted spoon, transfer the veal and vegetables to a heated serving dish. Keep warm. Strain the cooking liquid into a saucepan add the cream and boil over a high heat, until reduced by ⅓ and the consistency of thin cream. Adjust the seasoning.
8 Pour the sauce over the meat and vegetables. Sprinkle with snipped fresh chives and serve immediately.

 bringing to room temperature, then 1¾ hours   Chablis

Sauté potatoes

Serves 4
500–750 g /1–1½ lb even-sized potatoes
50–75 g /2–3 oz butter
15 ml /1 tbls olive oil
salt and freshly ground black pepper
30 ml /2 tbls finely chopped parsley (optional)

1 Peel and slice the potatoes thinly and soak them in cold water for a few minutes — this removes some of the starch and helps prevent them sticking later when they are fried. Drain and dry them thoroughly in kitchen paper or a clean tea towel.
2 Use butter for frying for the flavour it gives, plus a tiny amount of oil to prevent burning. Melt the butter and oil in two heavy frying-pans. When really hot, add the potatoes in a single layer, without overcrowding the pans. Sauté over a moderate heat, turning frequently with a spatula, until the potatoes are crisp and golden. Season to taste with salt and freshly ground black pepper towards the end of the cooking time, adding a little more butter if necessary.
3 Turn the potatoes onto a heated serving dish and serve sprinkled with finely chopped parsley, if you wish.

● This popular and frequently served dish is often very badly cooked. Undercooked hard potatoes or overcooked sauté potatoes are usually caused by overcrowding the potatoes in the pan. The potatoes must cook in a single layer, or the rising steam will moisten them instead of giving them that crisp golden finish.

If you have ever wondered how restaurants manage to produce perfect sauté potatoes ready to order, I can tell you that they start with completely cold baked potatoes in their jackets. This is easy to copy at home. Heat the fat until very hot and toss the peeled potato slices until they are golden, then season.

Orange and chicory salad

Serves 4
3 oranges
3 heads chicory
1 small crisp round lettuce
a pinch of cayenne pepper
45 ml /3 tbls olive oil
15 ml /1 tbls wine vinegar
salt and freshly ground black pepper
30 ml /2 tbls finely chopped fresh parsley
12 black olives, halved and stoned, to garnish

1 Peel the oranges, removing the white pith. Cut them into segments over a bowl to catch the juices, cutting down the side of each segment inside the membrane. Squeeze out any remaining juice from the scraps. Reserve the segments and all the juice.
2 Separate each head of chicory into leaves, discarding the tough core and any discoloured or damaged leaves. Wash well in cold water and drain thoroughly. Wrap in a clean tea-towel.
3 Wash the lettuce carefully, then pat each leaf dry with a clean cloth or absorbent paper. Use the prepared leaves to line 4 individual plates, or a large salad bowl.
4 Put a generous pinch of cayenne pepper into a small bowl, then slowly whisk in the olive oil. Beat in the vinegar, then the juices from the orange segments, until the mixture emulsifies. Season with salt and freshly ground black pepper, then stir in the chopped parsley.
5 If using individual plates, arrange the chicory leaves in a fan shape on top of the lettuce leaves, and place orange segments in the hollows of the leaves. Spoon the vinaigrette dressing over the salad and garnish each plate with the black olives. Alternatively, if using a salad bowl arrange the chicory leaves, orange segments and olives attractively on top of the lettuce leaves and spoon the dressing over them all.

 15 minutes preparation,
plus 15 minutes cooking

30 minutes

Choux cream puffs

Makes about 26 small puffs

50 g /2 oz butter, diced, plus
extra for greasing
5 ml /1 tsp sugar
65 g /2½ oz flour, sifted
2 eggs, beaten
a few drops of vanilla essence

For the Crème St Honoré
1 thin strip of orange zest
275 ml /10 fl oz milk

10 ml /2 tsp gelatine
4 egg yolks
125 g /4 oz sugar
25 g /1 oz flour
2.5 ml /½ tsp vanilla essence
4 egg whites

To serve
sifted icing sugar
strawberries

1   Heat the oven to 220C /425F /gas 7, and grease a baking sheet. To make the pastry, put the diced butter and sugar in a small, heavy saucepan, with 150 ml /5 fl oz cold water. Bring to the boil slowly.
2   When the liquid boils briskly, remove pan from heat. Quickly pour in all the flour at once and beat vigorously.
3   Return the pan to a low heat and continue to beat the paste for about 2 minutes until it forms itself into a smooth ball, leaving the bowl clean. Remove from the heat.
4   Add the eggs, a little at a time, beating vigorously. Continue to beat until the paste is glossy. Beat in the vanilla essence.
5   Fit a piping bag with an éclair nozzle and fill it with the pastry mixture. Pipe walnut-sized puffs onto the baking sheet, allowing plenty of space between each one.
6   Bake for 10 minutes, then remove the tray from the oven and reduce the heat to 190C /375F /gas 5. Pierce each puff in the side with a knife, return to the oven and bake for a further 10 minutes or until firm and dry. Leave the puffs to cool on a wire rack.
7   To make the Crème St Honoré, add the orange zest to the milk in a small pan and bring to the boil. Remove from the heat. Put the gelatine in 45 ml /3 tbls water to soften.
8   Whisk the egg yolks in a bowl over hot water until thick and pale. Gradually beat in the sugar and continue beating until the mixture is thick enough to form a ribbon trail when the spoon is lifted.
9   Discard the zest, then gradually pour the milk onto the yolk mixture, beating constantly. Beat in the flour. Strain into a saucepan.
10   Place the pan over moderate heat. Cook, stirring constantly, for 2–3 minutes, or until the custard thickens. Remove from the heat and stir in the softened gelatine until dissolved, and then the vanilla essence. Cool. Whisk the egg whites until stiff, then fold in.
11   To serve, split the little puffs almost in half. Pipe the cream into them and garnish with strawberries. Sift icing sugar on top.

2½ hours including
chilling

Cheeseboard

Cheese is usually served in Italy and France after the main course, so that the wine served with the meat course can be finished with the cheese. In Britain, when port is being served at the end of the meal, cheese is usually served after the dessert, as a savoury prelude to the port. But you may want to choose a wine specifically for a particular type of cheese and some suggestions are given below.

Bel paese
A soft but firm Italian cheese — its yellow-cream richness is mild and delicately flavoured — Bel paese is delicious with fruit. Although it is served almost exclusively as a dessert cheese, it can be used, if necessary, as a substitute for Mozzarella in certain cooked dishes. Bel paese keeps well, and its flavour tends to sharpen as it ages. As with all cheese, serve it at room temperature. A good companion wine would be Beaujolais, or a red or dry white Italian wine.

Brie
Talleyrand, the 19th century statesman and gourmet, called this soft creamy French cheese 'the king of cheeses'. Brie comes in thin, yellow crusted cartwheels dusted with a powdery white mould. It is delicious when soft and a little runny, but apt to be chalky when under-ripe. Brie smells of ammonia when past its prime. It is available by the slice, in individual wedge-shaped wooden boxes, or cut to order from the whole. Brie is at its mellow best as a dessert cheese; try it, too, as the flavour accent for cheese pastry. A good companion wine would be Corton, Pommard or Nuits St Georges.

Leicester
Crumbly and flaky, much like Cheshire cheese in texture, Leicester has a deep orange-red colour. This famous English cheese keeps well, but is at its best when young and mild. It can be served on a cheeseboard, is good with salads and is excellent as one of the components of Welsh rarebit. A good companion wine would be Beaujolais — or try it with ale, beer or cider.

Index